The Theology Program

Humanity & Sin

Copyright ©2011 Credo House Ministries
109 NW 142nd St., Suite B, Edmond, OK 73003

ISBN-13: 978-1460933251
ISBN-10: 1460933257

BISAC: Religion/Christian Theology/General

This material is provided for students and instructors in The Theology Program. Use of this material is encouraged for personal study and for use in preparation of lessons, sermons, or other oral communication. This material may be quoted so long as the material is unaltered and credit is given to The Theology Program. It may not under any circumstances be reprinted for any reason or any purpose without the prior expressed written consent of the Credo House Ministries.

Certified instructors in The Theology Program are allowed to add to the material so long as approval is granted by The Theology Program developers. Pastors and teachers are encouraged to use the material in their teaching, but it must remain unaltered.

Unless otherwise noted, Scriptures are taken from the NEW AMERICAN STANDARD BIBLE, ©Copyright The Lockman Foundation 1960, 1962, 1963, 1968, 1971, 1972, 1973, 1975, 1977, 1995. Used by permission. Scriptures are also taken from the NET Bible, © 1997–2003 by Biblical Studies Press, L.L.C. and the authors, and from HOLY BIBLE, NEW INTERNATIONAL VERSION®. Copyright © 1973, 1978, 1984 by International Bible Society. Used by permission of Zondervan Publishing House.

Credo House
PUBLISHERS
www.credohouse.org

Humanity and Sin

"What is man that You take thought of him,
And the son of man that You care for him?"
—Psalm 8:4

Question Outline

- Why did God create us?
- What is our essential nature?
- Is our body the same as our soul?
- Do we have both material and immaterial parts?
- Do we have a body, soul, and a spirit?
- Do we just have a body and a soul/spirit?
- What is Conditional Unity?
- What is Gnostic Dualism?
- When and how was our soul created?
- What does it mean to be born again?
- What does it mean to be created in the image of God?

- How did the Fall affect the imago Dei?
- What is Original Sin?
- How did the fall affect our will?
- What is the Pelagian view?
- What is the Arminian view?
- Do we really have a free will?
- How can we be held guilty for the sin of another?
- Men and women: How are we different?
- What is the Egalitarian view?
- What is the Complementarian view?

Course Outline

Syllabus 7

The Why of Man
Session 1: Why did God create man? 21

The What of Man
Session 2: Constitution of Man: Monism 29
Session 3: Constitution of Man: Dualism 41
Session 4: Creation of the Soul 61
Session 5: The Imago Dei in Humanity 69

The Fall of Man
Session 6: Original Sin: Pelagianism 77
Session 7: Original Sin: Augustinianism and Arminianism 85
Session 8: Free will 95

The Sex of Humanity
Session 9: Egalitarianism 107
Session 10: Complementarianism 115

Appendices
Appendix 1: Doctrine of Original Sin 125
Appendix 2: Council of Orange 136
Key Terms: 142

HUMANITY AND SIN
Syllabus

Course Description

This course is a study of the nature of humanity and sin. We will look at the nature of humanity from a biblical perspective by examining the pre-fall and post-fall state of man. We will see how these issues were dealt with from a historical perspective by spending much time on the debate between St. Augustine and Pelagius. Attempt will be made to understand the implications of man being created in the image of God. Debates about the origin and nature of sin will be examined by asking questions such as:

> What is sin?
> Where did it begin?
> Why did God allow it?
> Are there different types
> of sin?

Course Objectives

1. The student will struggle with the question, "Why did God create man?"

2. The student will gain knowledge of the different theories concerning human constitution.

3. The student will have a greater understanding of what it means to be created in the image of God.

4. The student will learn what affect the fall had on the mind of man as well as his moral, social, and volitional abilities.

5. The student will gain an appreciation of human dignity by learning that while man is not what he was supposed to be,

Course Textbooks

Required:

- Grudem, Wayne. Systematic Theology. Grand Rapids, MI: Zondervan, 1994.
- Olson, Roger. Mosaic of Christian Beliefs. Downers Grove, IL: IVP, 2002.
- Bible (preferably New American Standard or NET Bible)

Course Requirements and Grading

This course can be taken at two levels: Certificate or self-study.

1. Certificate Students: Certificate students take the course for a grade to receive a certificate that can be applied towards the TTP diploma. You must pay the tuition, attend or view all ten sessions, and complete enough of the homework according to the grading system below to receive a passing grade. This applies to both online and campus students.

2. Self-study: Self-study students take the course for enrichment only. Homework is not required, although doing homework will obviously enrich your learning from the course.

Continuing Education Units (CEUs) may be offered depending upon the venue. Ask your instructor for more information.

Honors credit can be earned in this course by completing all the coursework and completing an additional reading assigned by the teacher. See bibliography for options.

Assignment Description - see course schedule for due dates

Viewing/Attending classes: Students are required to attend or view all ten sessions of the course. (All sessions for every course are posted on the TTP website and are available for viewing or for purchase.) Online certificate students: It is preferred that you view only one session per week so you won't get too far ahead of the rest of the class.

SYLLABUS

While attending or viewing the sessions is required for all certificate students, it does not apply toward your grade and you cannot receive credit without it.

Ten hours of theological community time (online certificate students only): All online certificate students are required to spend one hour a week in the online TTP forums or in the voice/chat rooms provided. Each course will have a separate classroom in the TTP forums. In this classroom, you can accrue theological community time by asking or answering questions of other students, blogging your thoughts, discussing issues relevant to the course, or posting your answers to the discussion questions at the end of each lesson. Voice and chat rooms will be open each week where you can participate in live theological conversation with other students in your class (see website for details). While theological community time is required for all online certificate students, it does not apply toward your grade and you cannot receive credit without it.

1. Reading: Various reading assignments will be given during the ten-week period. Each student will be expected to read the material according to the ten-weeksession schedule provided in the syllabus.

2. Scripture memorization: Each student will memorize the passages provided on the Scripture memorization sheet in the syllabus. Once completed, the student will recite the memorized Scripture to a partner who will affirm the completion by signing the Scripture memorization sheet.

The preferred translations for all memorization in English are listed below:
- New American Standard
- NET Bible (available at www.bible.org)
- English Standard Version
- New International Version

3. Case Studies: The two case studies in the Student Notebook must be completed according to schedule. Online certificate students are to post their case studies online on the TTP forums. Your instructor will grade them online, marking them in red.

4. Vocabulary Quizzes: Two closed-book theological vocabulary quizzes will be given during the course of the semester. Online students can find these quizzes on the website. See schedule for due dates. Once the student looks at the quiz, he or she must take the quiz. In other words, you cannot look at the quiz, study the right terms, and then take the test.

Grading System

Complete 1 of 4	Complete 2 of 4	Complete 3 of 4	Complete 4 of 4	Complete all 4 plus honors reading
D	*C*	*B*	*A*	*A* *with honors*

Schedule

Session No.	Session Date	Session Topic	Assignments	Due Dates
1		Introduction to Course Why did God create man?	Reading Assignment: Grudem, 439-453	Session 2
2		Constitution of Man: Monism	Reading Assignment: Grudem, 472-489	Session 3
3		Constitution of Man: Dualism		Session 4
4		Creation of the Soul	Reading Assignment: *Mosaic of Christian Belief*, 199-222	Session 5
5		The *Imago Dei* in Humanity	Cast Study #1 Vocabulary Quiz #1	Session 6
6		Original Sin: Pelagianism	Appendix 1: "Original Sin" paper by Michael Patton	Session 7
7		Original Sin: Augustinianism	Reading Assignment: Grudem, 454-471 Appendix 2: Council of Orange	Session 8
8		Free Will		Session 9
9		Egalitarianism	Reading Assignment: Grudem, 490-514	Session 10
10		Complementarianism	Case Study #2 Vocabulary Quiz #2	One week after session 10

BIBLIOGRAPHY FOR HUMANITY AND SIN

Required Reading

Wayne Grudem, Systematic Theology. Grand Rapids, MI: Zondervan, 1994.

Roger Olsen, Mosaic of Christian Beliefs. Downers Grove, IL: IVP, 2002.

Essential Reading

Boyd, Gregory and Paul Eddy. Across the Spectrum. Grand Rapids, MI: Baker, 2002.

Brown, O.J. Heresies. Peabody, MA: Hendrickson, 1988.

Elwell, Walter A., ed. Evangelical Dictionary of Theology. Grand Rapids, MI: Baker Book House Company, 2001.

*Moreland, J. P. Love Your God with All Your Mind. Colorado Springs, CO: Nav Press, 1997.

Ryrie, Charles C. Basic Theology. Wheaton, IL: Victor Books, 1986.

Suggested Reading

Allen, Ronald B. The Majesty of Man: The Dignity of Being Human. Grand Rapids, MI:

Kregel Publications, 2000.

Berkhof, Louis. The History of Doctrine. Grand Rapids, MI: Baker, 1937.

Blocher, Henri. Orignial Sin: Illuminating the Riddle. Grand Rapids, MI: William B. Eerdmans Publishing Company, 1997.

Campbell, Iain D. The Doctrine of Sin. Fearn, Ross-shire, Great Britain: Christian Focus Publications, 1976.

Chafer, Lewis Sperry. Systematic Theology, Volumes 1, 2, 3, 4. Grand Rapids, MI: Kregel Publications, 1976.

Erickson, Millard J. Christian Theology. Grand Rapids, MI: Baker Book House Company, 1998.

Enns, Paul. The Moody Handbook of Theology. Chicago, IL: Moody Press, 1989.

Feinberg, John, Norman Geisler, Bruce Reichenbach, Clark Pinnock. Predestination &

Free Will. Downers Grove, IL: InterVarsity Press, 1986.

Gerstner, John H. A Primer on Free Will. Phillipsburg, NJ: Presbyterian and Reformed Publishing Company, 1982.

Hodge, Charles. Systematic Theology, Three Volume Set. Peabody, MA: Hendrickson Publishers, 2001.

House, H. Wayne. Charts of Christian Theology & Doctrine. Grand Rapids, MI: Zondervan, 1992.

Machen, J. Gresham. The Christian View of Man. Carlisle, PA: The Banner of Truth Trust, 1965.

Moreland, J.P. and William Lane Craig. Philosophical Foundations for a Biblical Worldview. Downers Gove, IL: IVP, 2003. (Christian Philosophy and Anthropology)

Piper, John and Wayne Grudem. Recovering Biblical Manhood and Womanhood. Wheaton, IL: Crossway Books, 1991.

Plantinga, Jr., Cornelius. A Breviary of Sin. Grand Rapids, MI: William B. Eerdmans Publishing Company, 1995.

*Pratt, Jr., Richard L. Designed for Dignity: What God Has Made It Possible For You To Be. Phillipsburg, NJ: Presbyterian and Reformed Publishing Company, 2000.

Pyne, Robert A. Humanity & Sin: The Creation, Fall and Redemption of Humanity. Nashville, TN: Word Publishing, 1999.

Roberts, Linleigh J. Let Us Make Man. Carlisle, PA: The Banner of Truth Trust, 1988.

Sherlock, Charles. The Doctrine of Humanity: Contours of Christian Theology. Downers Grove, IL: InterVarsity Press, 1996.

Smith, David L. With Willful Intent: A Theology of Sin. Wheaton, IL: Victor Books, 1994.

*Sproul, R.C. Willing to Believe: The Controversy Over Free Will. Grand Rapids, MI: Baker Books, 1997.

Walton, Robert. Charts of Church History. Grand Rapids, MI: Zondervan, 1986.

Honors Reading

Read one book marked with an asterisk (*).

Student Name _____

SCRIPTURE MEMORIZATION SHEET

The Purpose of Humanity

1 Corinthians. 10:31
The imago Dei:
Genesis. 1:26-27
James. 3:8-9

The Constitution of Man

2 Corinthians. 5:6-9

The Fall of Man

1 Corinthians. 2:14
John. 8:34
Psalm. 51:5

I _____ have listened to _____ and confirm that he or she has recited the above Scriptures to me without any aid.

Signature_____

CASE STUDY 1: WHAT IS MAN?
Humanity and Sin

This is to be a "real life" case study. Find a person who is willing to sit and talk to you for thirty minutes to one hour. This person may or may not be a Christian. This might be a family member, a co-worker, someone at the gym, or even someone from church.

With notes in hand, you are to teach what you have learned in Humanity and Sin class concerning the constitution of humanity.

These are the issues that need to be covered:

- Cover these questions before you begin:
    1. Do you think that man has an immaterial and material part?
    2. If so, what is the immaterial part?
    3. When does a person gain this immaterial part (e.g., conception, birth, "age of accountability"?)
- After this, you are to go through the different theories about the constitution of man covered in class. (Refer to your notes.) Be sure to explain the significance of the body.
- Finally, you are to explain the different theories concerning the creation of the soul. Demonstrate the relevance of this topic to the current issue of abortion. The object of this assignment is to present the different views of man. Your goal here is not to convince someone of your particular persuasion, but to help people to understand the importance of thinking through these issues.

After you are done, write a half page to a page summary of the encounter and hand it in. Online student are to post their summary in their class forum. Grades will be based upon the completion of the assignment, not the effectiveness of the presentation. Everyone who completes this will receive credit for the case study.

CASE STUDY 2: ORIGINAL SIN
Humanity and Sin

This is to be a "real life" case study. Find a person who is willing to sit and talk to you for thirty minutes to one hour. This person may or may not be a Christian. This might be a family member, a co-worker, someone at the gym, or even someone from church.

With notes in hand, you are to teach what you have learned in Humanity and Sin class concerning the doctrine of the Fall of Man.

- Cover these questions before you begin:
    1. Do you think that man is essentially good or essentially evil? Why?
    2. When you hear the term "original sin" what do you think?
    3. In what way do you think the sin of Adam affects us?

- After this, go through the different theories about the fall. Explain the difference between Augustinianism and Pelagianism.

- Then, use your notes to explain what the Bible has to say about original sin.

- Then ask if they think that it is fair that we are held guilty for the sin of another.

- Explain to them the federal headship view as it relates to imputed sin. Use St.Thomas Aquinas' angel illustration.

The object of this assignment is to present a logical and biblical argument for the doctrine of the Trinity. Your goal here is not to convince someone of the truth (although that would be great), but simply to present the arguments clearly.

After you are done, write a half page to a page summary of the encounter and hand it in. Online student are to post their summary in their class forum. Grades will be based upon the completion of the assignment, not the effectiveness of the presentation. Everyone who completes this will receive credit for the case study.

HUMANITY AND SIN

Monism
Determinalism
Free Will
Egalitarianism
Personal Sin
Arminianism
Mortal Sin
Pelagianism
Original sin
Gnostic Dualism
Anthropology
Traducianism
ORIGINAL SIN
Imago Dei
Compatibilism
Complementarian
Augustinianism

Session 1

WHY DID GOD CREATE MAN?
Does God need us?

Questions:

- What was God's motivation in creating man?
- Was God in need of companionship?
- Did God need to be worshiped?

Anthropology: Gk. anthropos, "Man"

> "The scientific study of the origin, the behavior, and the physical, social, and cultural development of humans."
>
> —American Heritage Dictionary

Definition of Anthropology: The study of the purpose and nature of humanity both, in its pre-fall and post-fall state.

Why study the Doctrine of Humanity?

1. It significantly affects every other doctrine of theology.
2. It shapes your views on sociology, politics, and the family.
3. It will affect your views of psychology.
4. Humanity is something about which everyone has expressed views.
5. It will affect how you minister to both believers and to non-believers.
6. It affects how you view yourself.

> "How you answer the question concerning the significance of being human will determine your views about what inherent rights people have, how people should be governed, and what authority, if any, they have to treat animals differently than they treat people.
>
> "Indeed, how you answer these questions will greatly affect your views on whether it is legal to allow severely deformed babies to die, whether people have the right or responsibility to take others off life support, whether and when people have the right to choose abortion, and whether human cloning should be pursued."
>
> —Gregory Boyd
>
> _{Gregory Boyd and Paul Eddy, *Across the Spectrum*, (Grand Rapids, MI 2002), 74-75.}

Why did God create man?

> Question 1: What is the chief and highest end of man?
> Answer: Man's chief and highest end is to glorify God and enjoy him forever.
> —Westminster Larger Catechism

> "We hold these truths to be self-evident, that all men are created equal, that they are endowed by their Creator with certain unalienable rights, that among these are life, liberty, and the pursuit of happiness."
> —U.S. Declaration of Independence

> "It's not about you."
> —Rick Warren
>
> _{*The Purpose Driven Life* (Grand Rapids, MI: Zondervan, 2002), 17.}

SESSION 1: WHY DID GOD CREATE MAN?

Wrong:

1. God did not create man (naturalism).

2. Man is an eternal extension of who and what God is (pantheism/panentheism).

3. Man is eternal as God is eternal (pantheism/polytheism).

4. God needed help with his new creation.

5. God was in need of a companion.

Genesis 1:1–2, 26–31; 2:7–9, 15–25

Psalm 8:3–6

"When I consider Your heavens, the work of Your fingers, the moon and the stars, which You have ordained; what is man that You take thought of him, and the son of man that You care for him? Yet You have made him a little lower than God, and You crown him with glory and majesty! You make him to rule over the works of Your hands; you have put all things under his feet."

Job 7:17–18
"What is man that You magnify him, and that You are concerned about him, that You examine him every morning and try him every moment?"

1 Corinthians 10:31
"Whether, then, you eat or drink or whatever you do, do all to the glory of God."

1 Peter 4:11
"Whoever speaks, let it be with God's words. Whoever serves, do so with the strength that God supplies, so that in everything God will be glorified through Jesus Christ. To him belong the glory and the power forever and ever. Amen."

Romans 8:17, 30
"And if children, heirs also, heirs of God and fellow heirs with Christ, if indeed we suffer with Him so that we may also be glorified with Him."
"And those he predestined, he also called; and those he called, he also justified; and those he justified, he also glorified."

Daniel 12:3
"Those who have insight will shine brightly like the brightness of the expanse of heaven, and those who lead the many to righteousness, like the stars forever and ever."

Ephesians 1:11b
"Having been predestined according to His purpose who works all things after the counsel of His will."

Is the Bible obscure or clear as to the motivation behind the creation of man? Why?

Right:

    1. Because God is a creative God.

    2. So that man would be able to glorify God.

    3. So that God would be able to share His glory with others.

    4. To accomplish His will unto whatever end.

SESSION I: WHY DID GOD CREATE MAN?

GROUP DISCUSSION QUESTIONS:

1. In the lesson, the statement was made that understanding the doctrine of humanity is as important as studying the doctrine of God. In what ways might this be true?

2. In the lecture, it was said that the doctrine of humanity will greatly affect the way you vote. Discuss further how this might be true with regards to various political issues (e.g., abortion, social security, foreign affairs).

3. How important it the question: Why did God create man? Please explain.

4. Why do you think that God, in the Bible, is not more explicit as to why He created man?

5. Read these passages:

   Psalm 8:3–6
   "When I consider Your heavens, the work of Your fingers, the moon and the stars, which You have ordained; what is man that You take thought of him, and the son of man that You care for him? Yet You have made him a little lower than God, and You crown him with glory and majesty! You make him to rule over the works of Your hands; you have put all things under his feet."

   Job 7:17–18
   "What is man that You magnify him, and that You are concerned about him, that You examine him every morning and try him every moment?"
   In what ways did this lesson help you to better identify with that which Job and David are expressing?

   In what ways did this lesson help you to better identify with that which Job and David are expressing?

SESSION 1: WHY DID GOD CREATE MAN?

6. Briefly discuss how these passages contribute answers to the question: "Why did God make man?"

> **Psalm 50:7–12**
> "He says: "Listen my people! I am speaking! Listen Israel! I am accusing you! I am God, your God! I am not condemning you because of your sacrifices, or because of your burnt sacrifices that you continually offer me. I do not need to take a bull from your household or goats from your sheepfolds. For every wild animal in the forest belongs to me, as well as the cattle that graze on a thousand hills. I keep track of every bird in the hills, and the insects of the field are mine. Even if I were hungry, I would not tell you, for the world and all it contains belong to me."
>
> **Acts 17:24–25**
> "The God who made the world and everything in it, who is Lord of heaven and earth, does not live in temples made by human hands, nor is he served by human hands, as if he needed anything, because he himself gives life and breath and everything to everyone."
>
> **Job 41:11**
> [God speaking] "Who has confronted me that I should repay? Everything under heaven belongs to me."

7. The Doctrine of Aseity asserts that God is not, nor ever has been in need of anything. In what ways do you think that we misrepresent God's aseity when we say that God created us in order that He could be worshiped and glorified?

8. How was your thinking most challenged by this lesson? Please explain.

Session 2

THE CONSTITUTION OF MAN: MONISM

What Exactly Did God Create?

Outline for the "What of Man":

A. The Constitution of Man : Monism
B. The Constitution of Man: Dualism
C. The Creation of the Soul
D. The Imago Dei in Man

Questions:

- What does it mean to be human?
- When you die, what happens to you?
- Is there such a thing as a soul?
- What, if any, is the distinction between the soul and the spirit?
- What is the relationship between the body and the soul?
- What is our essential nature?

The Constitution of Man

Words that the Bible uses with reference to the constitution of man:

Body	σωμα *soma*	1 Corinthians 6:19
Soul	ψυχη *psuche*	Matthew 16:26
Spirit	πνευμα *pneuma*	1 Corinthians 2:11
Mind	νους *nous* διανοια *dianoia*	Romans 12:2 Mark 12:30
Heart	καρδια *cardia*	Mark 12:30
Flesh	σαρξ *sarx*	Matt. 26:41
Gut, bowels	σπλαγχνον *splagchnon*	Philippians. 1:8

Two Main Alternatives:

    1. Physicalism
    2. Dualism

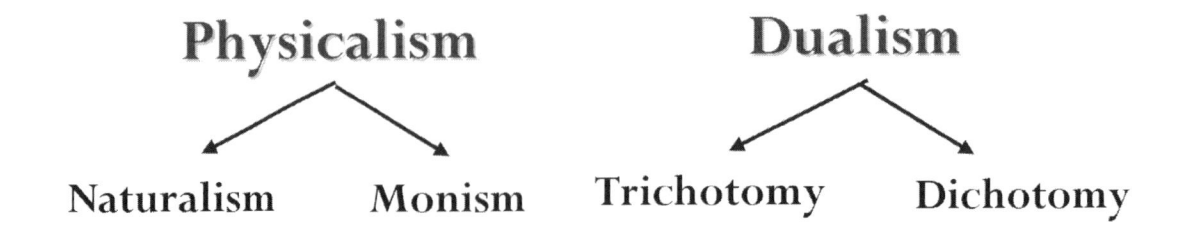

Physicalism
- Naturalism
- Monism

Dualism
- Trichotomy
- Dichotomy

SESSION 2: THE CONSTITUTION OF MAN: MONISM

Views Held by Christians:

1. Monism

2. Dualism
    - Trichotomy
    - Dichotomy

Is our body the same as our soul?

Definition: Gk. monos, "one" or "alone." The teaching that the spirit, soul, and body are all essentially the same or that the spirit and soul do not exist without the body. This often goes by the name "soul sleep."

Adherents: Jehovah's Witnesses, Christian Scientists, Christadelphians, J.A.T. Robertson, neo-orthodoxy

> "The souls that do depart hence do sleep, being without all sense, feeling, and perceiving until the day of judgment, do utterly decent from the right that is closed to us in Holy Scriptures."
> —King Henry VI

Monism — Body

Trichotomy — Body, Soul, Spirit

Dichotomy — Body, Soul/Spirit

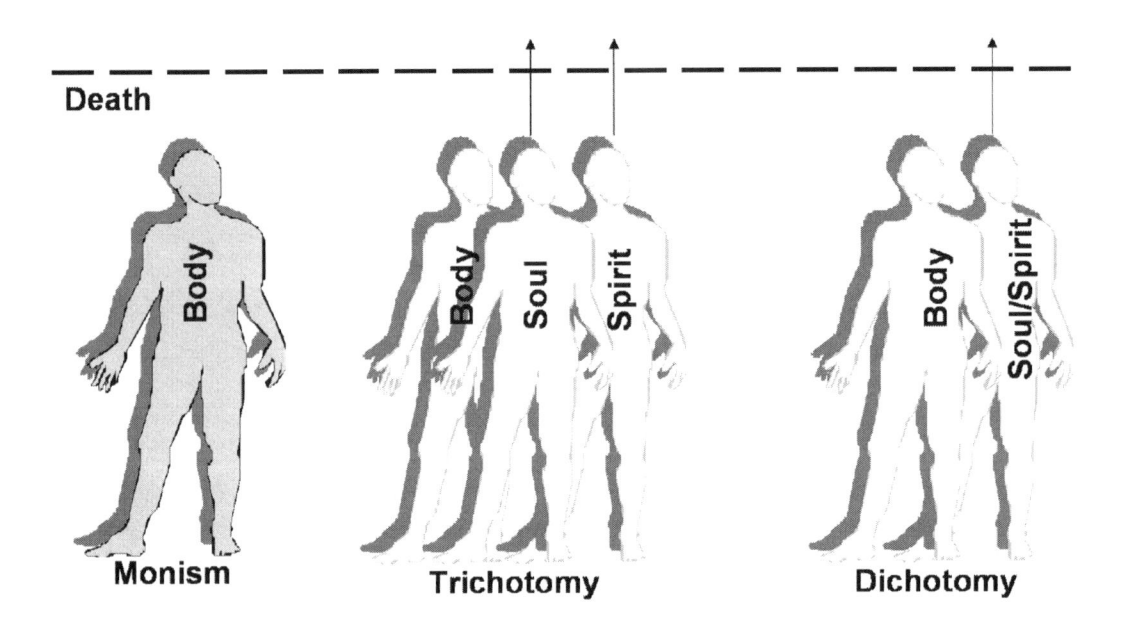

Defense of Monism:

1. When the Bible speaks of death, it speaks in terms of sleeping.

> **Acts 13:36**
> "For David, after he had served the purpose of God in his own generation, fell asleep, and was laid among his fathers and underwent decay."

> **1 Thessalonians. 4:13–15**
> "But we do not want you to be uninformed, brethren, about those who are asleep, so that you will not grieve as do the rest who have no hope. For if we believe that Jesus died and rose again, even so God will bring with Him those who have fallen asleep in Jesus. For this we say to you by the word of the Lord, that we who are alive and remain until the coming of the Lord, will not precede those who have fallen asleep."

2. Those in the Old Testament showed no sign of belief in an intermediate state. They simply spoke of going to the place where all the dead go—the grave—which was called "Sheol." Their hope was only in the resurrection.

SESSION 2: THE CONSTITUTION OF MAN: MONISM

Job 17:13–16
"If I look for Sheol as my home, I make my bed in the darkness; if I call to the pit,
'You are my father;' To the worm, 'my mother and my sister;' Where now is my hope? And who regards my hope? Will it go down with me to Sheol? Shall we together go down into the dust?"

Genesis 50:25
"Then Joseph made the sons of Israel swear, saying, 'God will surely take care of you, and you shall carry my bones up from here.'"

3. Many biblical writers explicitly say that there is no intermediate state.

Psalm 6:5
"For there is no mention of You in death; in Sheol who will give You thanks?"

Psalm 30:9
"What profit is there in my blood, if I go down to the pit? Will the dust praise You? Will it declare Your faithfulness?"

Psalm 88:3–5
"For my soul has had enough troubles, and my life has drawn near to Sheol. I am reckoned among those who go down to the pit; I have become like a man without strength, forsaken among the dead, like the slain who lie in the grave, whom You remember no more, and they are cut off from Your hand."

Isaiah 38:18
"For Sheol cannot thank You, death cannot praise You; those who go down to the pit cannot hope for Your faithfulness."

Ecclesiastes 9:5, 10
"For the living know they will die; but the dead do not know anything, nor have they any longer a reward, for their memory is forgotten."
"Whatever your hand finds to do, do it with all your might; for there is no activity or planning or knowledge or wisdom in Sheol where you are going."

4. The idea of an intermediate state is of Greek origin. The Hebrews believed in a holistic self in which the hope was in the resurrection. The Greeks downplayed the role of the body/material self, believing that death was a release from this confinement. Those who see a plurality in the constitution of human nature read the Bible through Hellenistic (Greek) eyes, failing to see that when the Bible speaks of the body, soul, and spirit, it is the same as when it speaks of the mind, heart, and soul—they are all the same.

5. Modern science has demonstrated that there is a one to one correspondence between the neurological activity of the brain and the feelings, memories, personalities, and attitudes of a person. This makes the existence of the soul/spirit not only unnecessary, but untenable. Once the brain ceases activity, the person ceases to exist.

> "The evidence that we have indicates that our mental life is *dependant* on certain bodily processes, particularly those associated with the brain. We know, for example, that damage to various parts of the brain results in the cessation of certain kinds of conscious states—memories, thought processes, and the like. It seems eminently reasonable to infer from this that consciousness is dependent for its existence on the existence and proper function of the human brain. When at death the brain ceases to function, the reasonable inference is that our mental life ceases as well."
>
> —William Rowe
>
> Philosophy of Religion: An Introduction (Encino, CA: Dickenson, 1978), 141

Response to Monism:

1. Sleep is a metaphor that is often used for death. This does not mean that the whole person is asleep, just the body.

2. Monism is a misunderstanding in the nature of progressive revelation. Old Testament saints did not have as much revelation as we do. Therefore, while it is true that they had very little knowledge of an intermediate state, this does not rule out the possibility of its existence any more than having no knowledge of the new Heaven and the new Earth rules out the possibility of their future existence.

3. While knowledge of the intermediate state was obscure in the Old Testament, these biblical writers do not say that there is no intermediate state. Their message is about what people can not do in the intermediate state. The basic message is that after we die, we cannot proclaim knowledge, wisdom, and praise to others on Earth about what the Lord has done.

4. While it may be true that our ideas of the intermediate state could have Greek influence, it is not true that this makes it wrong. This is committing the genetic fallacy of ascribing falsehood to an idea because of its source. Besides this, the New Testament is the primary source of this view, not Greek philosophy.

5. While it is true that the brain is intricately linked to all aspects of a whole person, this does not prove that it is the whole person. The body is part of what a person is, but this does not necessarily mean that it is all that a person is.

Window Illustration

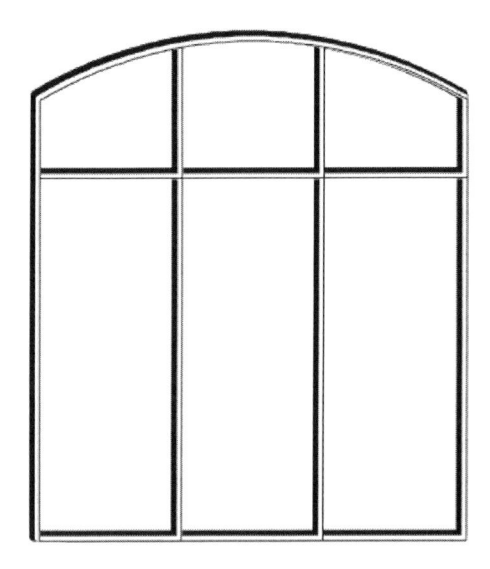

Do we have both material and immaterial parts?

SESSION 2: THE CONSTITUTION OF MAN: MONISM

GROUP DISCUSSION QUESTIONS

1. Read Matthew 15:10–20 (refer also to Jeremiah 17:9). Christ described the "heart" as the "part" of man that houses and produces defilement and sin. Did Christ mean that the heart has a separate cognitive ability other than that of the brain? If not, what did He mean?

2. Read Matthew 26:41. People often equate the "flesh," as used in Scripture, with the body. Is the flesh the same thing as the body? If not what is it?

3. The teaching that equates the "flesh" with the body was the teaching of an early heresy known as Gnosticism. Gnostics taught that everything physical was evil and everything spiritual is good (dualism). With regard to Christ, Gnostics thought that He only seemed to have a body, but He really did not. For if He did, He would be sinful. A.) If the flesh is the same thing as the body, how do you explain that Christ had a body? B.) If the flesh is the same thing as the body, how do you explain that people will one day have their bodies raised from the dead (read 1 Corinthians 15:20–23)? Discuss both

4. Do you believe that outbursts of anger produced by irritability are sinful? (Answer before moving on).

Modern medicine is advanced to the point that a pill can affect the chemical reactions in the brain to reduce irritability. This results in reducing anger. In this sense, sin can be controlled to a certain degree by medication. Do you agree? Discuss.

Hypothetically speaking, what if modern medicine produced a pill that would affect a person's ability to believe in God for those who skeptical by nature?

Would this be morally acceptable?

If such a pill were produced, would you encourage a skeptical family member to take it?

Why or why not?

5. Why do you think that God did not inform people in the Old Testament about the intermediate state?

SESSION 2: THE CONSTITUTION OF MAN: MONISM

6. The doctrine of Progressive Revelation teaches that God did not immediately inform humanity of all truth, but that He progressively gives truth in increments through the ages. Christians often think that because all biblical writers have correct doctrine, they also have complete doctrine. Discuss the fallacies of this.

7. What are some other Scriptural examples of things revealed to later saints that was unknown to earlier saints?

8. How does the doctrine of Progressive Revelation affect the arguments of Monism and Dualism? Please discuss.

9. How was your thinking most challenged by this lesson? Please explain.

Session 3

THE CONSTITUTION OF MAN: DUALISM

Questions:

- What does it mean to be human?
- When you die, what happens to "you"?
- Is there such a thing as a soul?
- What, if any, is the distinction between the soul and the spirit?
- What is the relationship between the body and the soul?

Dualism   The understanding that the constitution of man is pluralistic in nature, since there is an intermediate state of existence to which the immaterial/immortal part(s) of man goes to await the resurrection.

Adherents: Most of Orthodox Christianity.

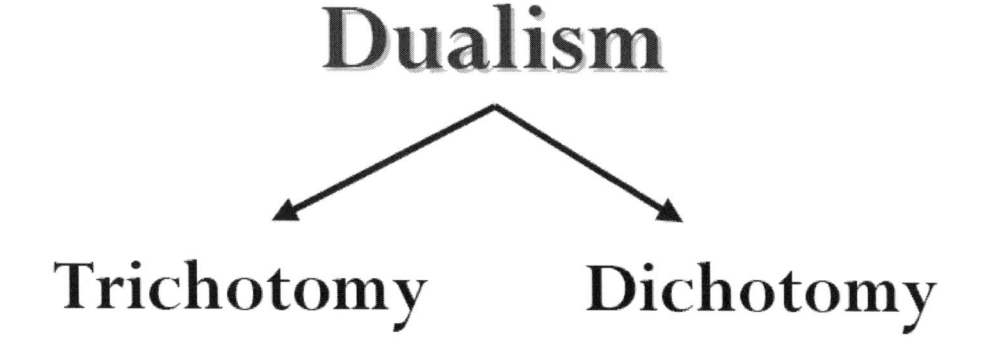

Dualism

Trichotomy   Dichotomy

Defense of Dualism:

1. That there is an intermediate state of existence between death and the resurrection is explicitly taught in Scripture.

Luke 23:42–43
"And he was saying, 'Jesus, remember me when You come into Your kingdom!' And He said to him, 'Truly I say to you, today you shall be with Me in Paradise.'"

2 Corinthians 5:6–8
"Therefore, being always of good courage, and knowing that while we are at home in the body we are absent from the Lord—for we walk by faith, not by sight—we are of good courage, I say, and prefer rather to be absent from the body and to be at home with the Lord."

Matthew. 10:28
"Do not fear those who kill the body but are unable to kill the soul; but rather fear Him who is able to destroy both soul and body in hell."

James. 2:26
"For just as the body without the spirit is dead, so also faith without works is dead."

Philippians 1:23–24
"But I am hard-pressed from both directions, having the desire to depart and be with Christ, for that is very much better; yet to remain on in the flesh is more necessary for your sake."

Luke 16:19–31
The story of the rich man and Lazarus.

SESSION 3: THE CONSTITUTION OF MAN: DUALISM

Revelation 6:9
"When the Lamb broke the fifth seal, I saw underneath the altar the souls of those who had been slain because of the word of God, and because of the testimony which they had maintained; and they cried out with a loud voice, saying, 'How long, O Lord, holy and true, will You refrain from judging and avenging our blood on those who dwell on the earth?'"

1 Samuel 28:11–15
Speaks of Samuel returning from the dead in spirit form to talk to Saul.

2. Knowledge of life after death is an anthropological axiom which has been common to all people of all time. People realize that the self, the "I" or "me," is something that transcends the brain or body. This cannot be dismissed easily.

3. Ceasing to exist at death and beginning to exist again at the resurrection amounts to God recreating us. Therefore, it would not really be "us" at all. We would not really have anything to look forward to in the afterlife, since "we" would not be involved in it. It would just be exact replicas of us.

4. Many people have had what is known as "near-death experiences." There is a common consistency among these experiences which makes them difficult to discount too easily (i.e., bright light, floating sensation, ability to hear what is going on around ones body even though there is no brain activity).

Response to Dualism

1. The Scriptures do not refer to hope in an intermediate state, but to the hope of the resurrection. We will be "present" with the Lord at the resurrection. The souls crying out to God do not need to be taken literally any more than when God says the blood of Abel is crying out to him (Gen. 4:9).

2. Universal knowledge or belief in something does not mean it is true.

3. While it may be difficult to envision and understand that God will recreate us at the resurrection, this does not mean that it is not true. It is also difficult to know how God will remake our bodies during the resurrection. Yet those who reject monism believe that they will be in the same bodies.

4. Near-death experiences are difficult to verify and border on the occult. Many of the testimonies of people are unbiblical since both believers and non-believers say they experience "going to a bright light."

Do we have a body, soul, and spirit?

Trichotomy — Gk. trikha, "three parts," and temno, "to cut." The teaching that man is made up of three essential parts: body, soul, and spirit.

   Body: All that is physical.
   Soul: Reason, emotions, will, memories, personality, dispositions.
   Spirit: The seat of our being, that which relates to God.

Adherents: Clement of Alexandria, Origen, Gregory of Nyssa, Watchman

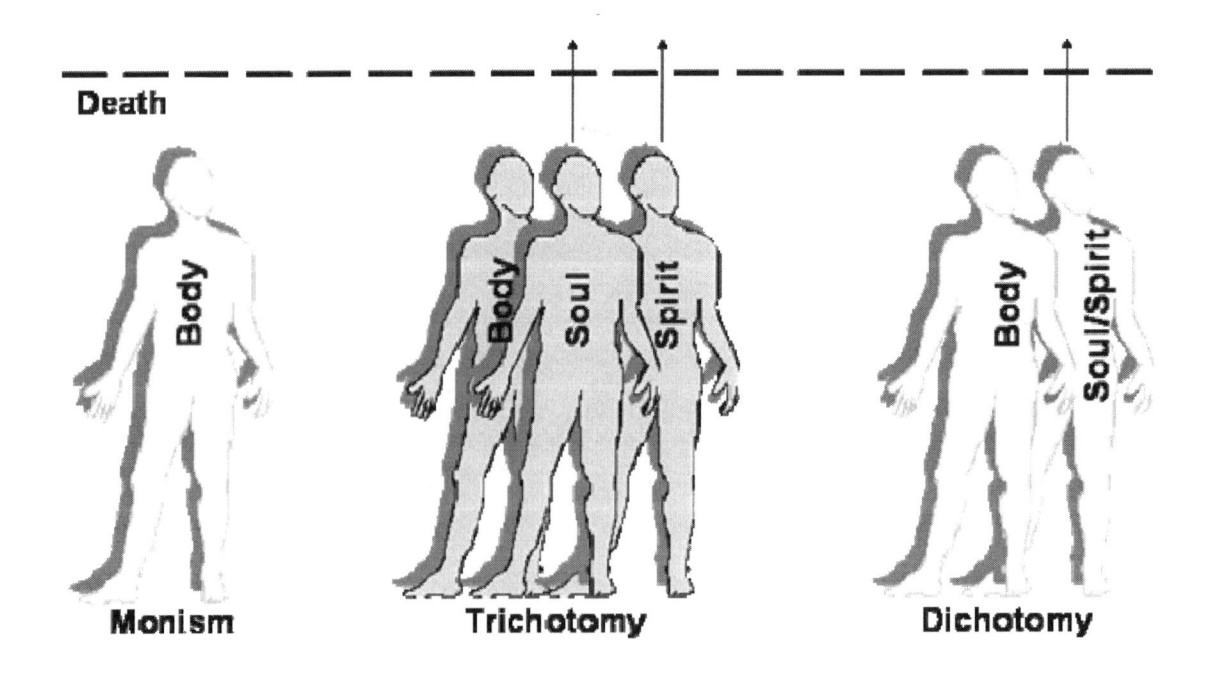

Death

Monism — Body

Trichotomy — Body, Soul, Spirit

Dichotomy — Body, Soul/Spirit

SESSION 3: THE CONSTITUTION OF MAN: DUALISM

BODY

SOUL

SPIRIT

Defense of Trichotomy:

1. Trichotomy is supported by Scripture.

   1 Thessalonians 5:23
   "Now may the God of peace Himself sanctify you entirely; and may your spiritand soul and body be preserved complete, without blame at the coming of our Lord Jesus Christ."

   Hebrews 4:12
   For the word of God is living and active and sharper than any two-edged sword, and piercing as far as the division of soul and spirit, of both joints and marrow, and able to judge the thoughts and intentions of the heart."

2. We are made in the image of a Trinitarian God. This image is best understood as trichotomy.

3. The spirit is presented in Scripture as the part of man that relates to God, unlike the body or the soul.

> **Genesis 2:17**
> "But from the tree of the knowledge of good and evil you shall not eat, for in the day that you eat from it you will surely die."
>
> **Ephesians 2:1**
> "And you were dead in your trespasses and sins."
>
> **Romans 8:10**
> "If Christ is in you, though the body is dead because of sin, yet the spirit is alive because of righteousness."

Response to Trichotomy:

1. The Bible often uses descriptive terms to speak of the different aspects of man's nature. This does not necessitate a constitutional division of the person. For example, does Mark 12:30 promote a four-fold division of the constitution of man?

"Love the Lord your God with all your heart and with all your soul and with all your mind and with all your strength."

2. If it were true that the composition of man reflects the plurality of the Trinity, then each component—body, soul, and spirit—is a separate person. The comparison with the Trinity is not consistent and carries no weight.

3. The word "dead" is being taken too literally. To be dead simply means to be separate from. Our entire being is separate from God as a result of the fall. Therefore, our entire being is dead, not just the spirit.

SESSION 3: THE CONSTITUTION OF MAN: DUALISM

Do we have just a body and a soul/spirit?

Dichotomy Gk. dicha, "two parts" and temno, "to cut." The teaching that man is made up of two essential parts: material (body), and nonmaterial (soul/spirit).

Material: All that is physical.
Non-material: Spirit, soul

Adherents: Augustine, John Calvin, Hodge, most of historic orthodox Christianity.

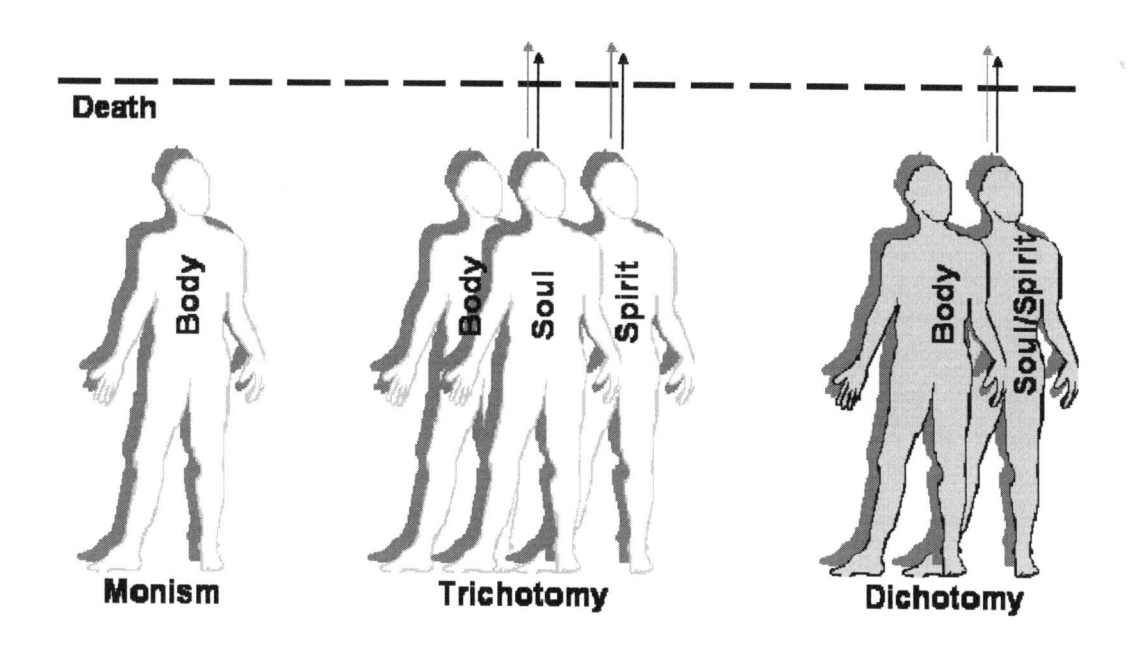

Death

Monism — Body

Trichotomy — Body, Soul, Spirit

Dichotomy — Body, Soul/Spirit

Defense of Dichotomy:

1. Unless the Scripture explicitly teaches that the immaterial part of man is a plurality, it should be assumed that it is one.

2. When there seems to be a distinction made in Scripture between the soul and spirit, it is not an ontological distinction but a functional distinction. It can be compared to our modern day distinction between the heart and the mind. For example, someone may say that they have accepted something with their mind, but their heart cannot accept it. They are not saying that their heart has a separate cognitive function other than their mind, but that a certain aspect of their mind (i.e. emotion) cannot accept it.

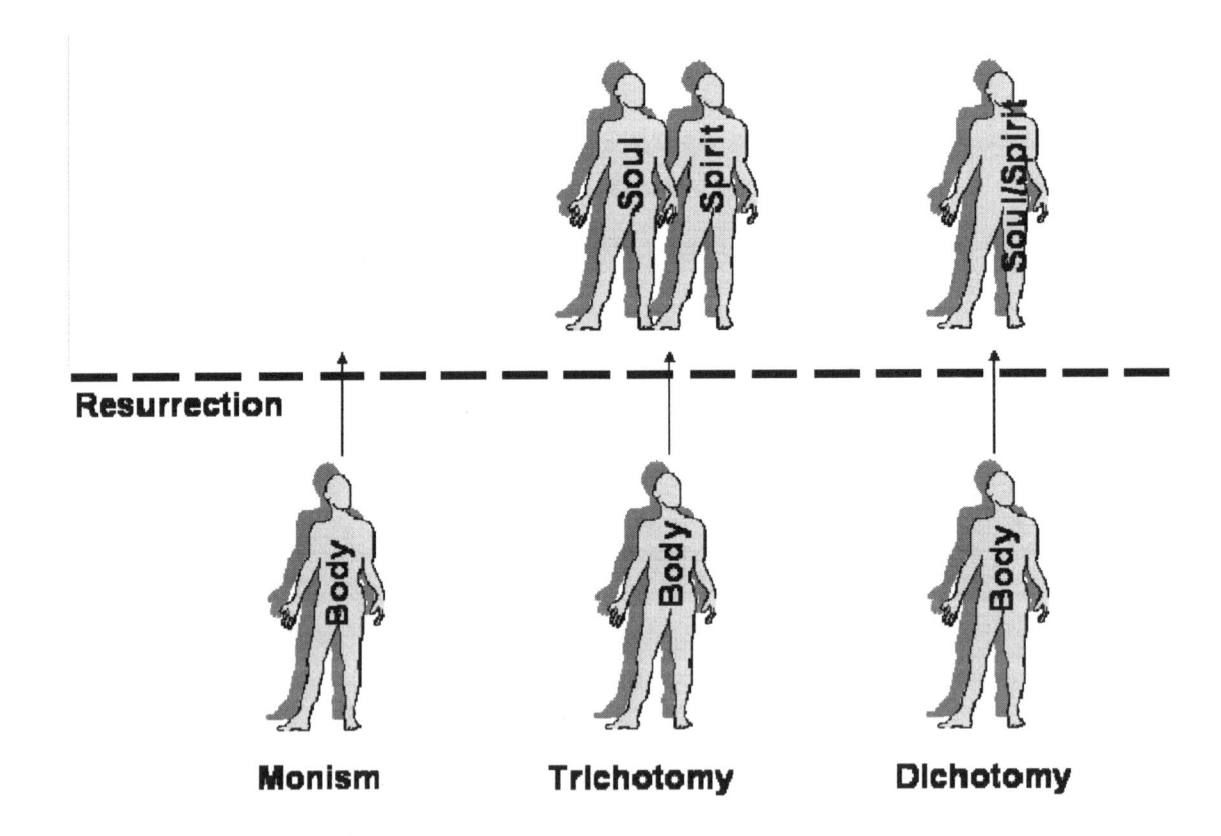

SESSION 3: THE CONSTITUTION OF MAN: DUALISM

What is Conditional Unity?

Conditional Unity This position affirms both the essential unity of the material and immaterial part of man and the existence of an intermediate state. A person does not have a body and a soul, but is a body and a soul, neither of which alone make up the whole person.

Adherents: Millard Erickson, Anthony Hoekema, Charles Sherlock

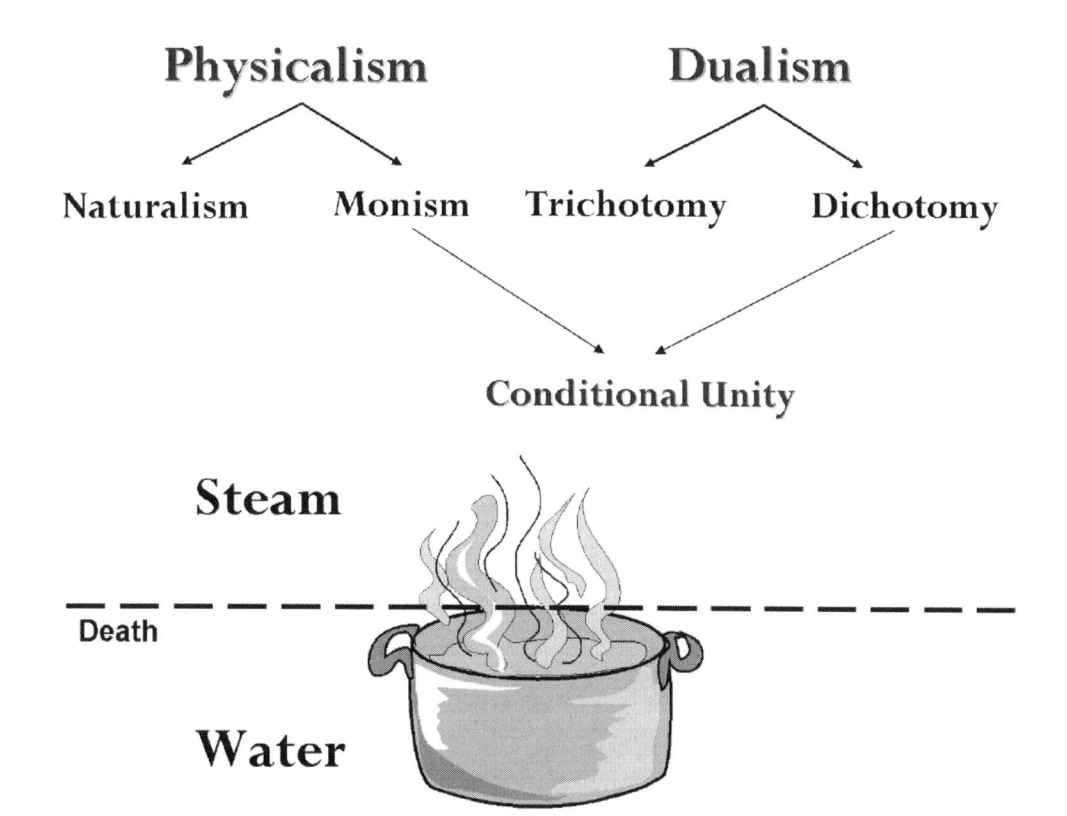

Physicalism → Naturalism, Monism

Dualism → Trichotomy, Dichotomy

→ **Conditional Unity**

Steam

--- Death ---

Water

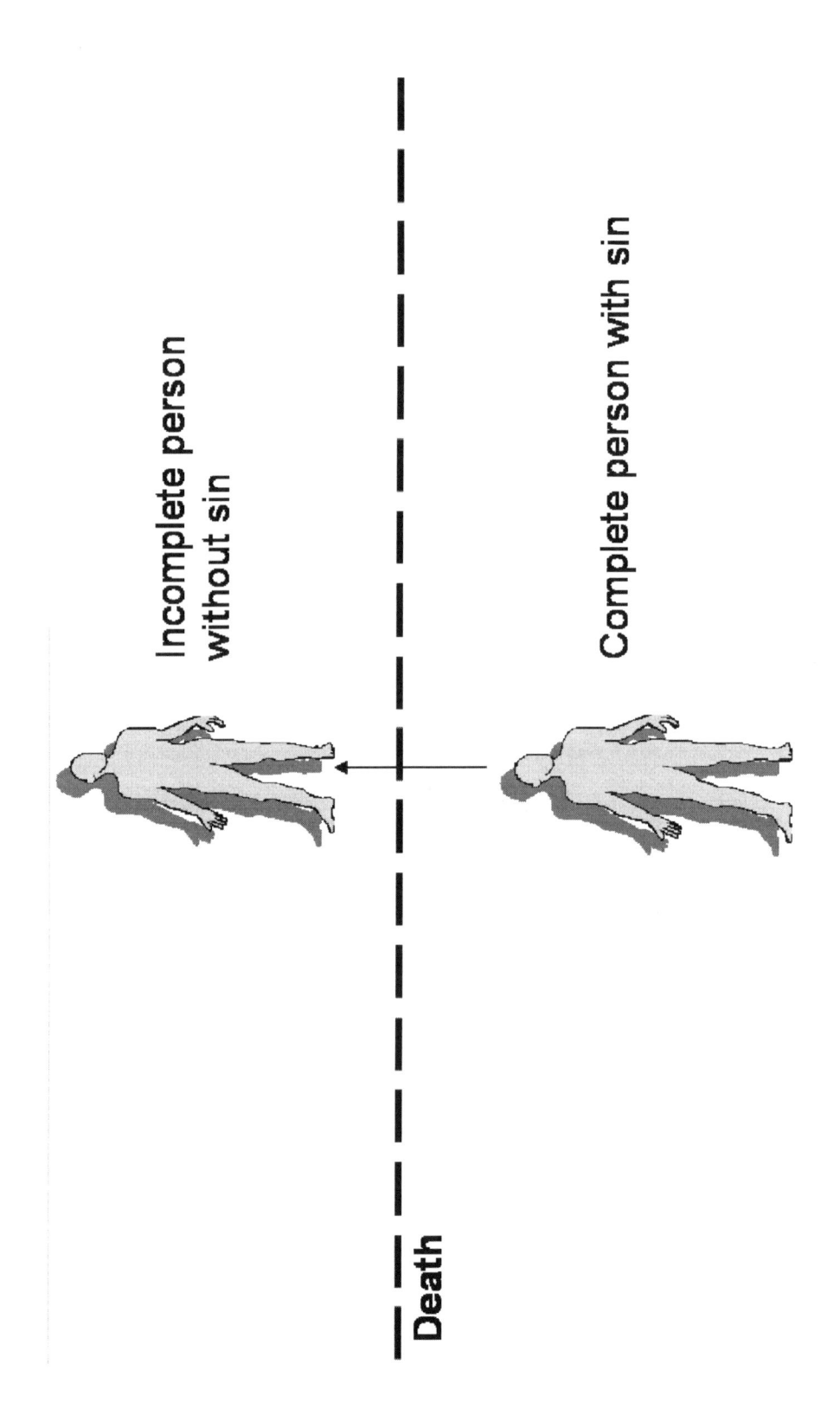

Complete person with sin → Incomplete person without sin

Death

SESSION 3: THE CONSTITUTION OF MAN: DUALISM

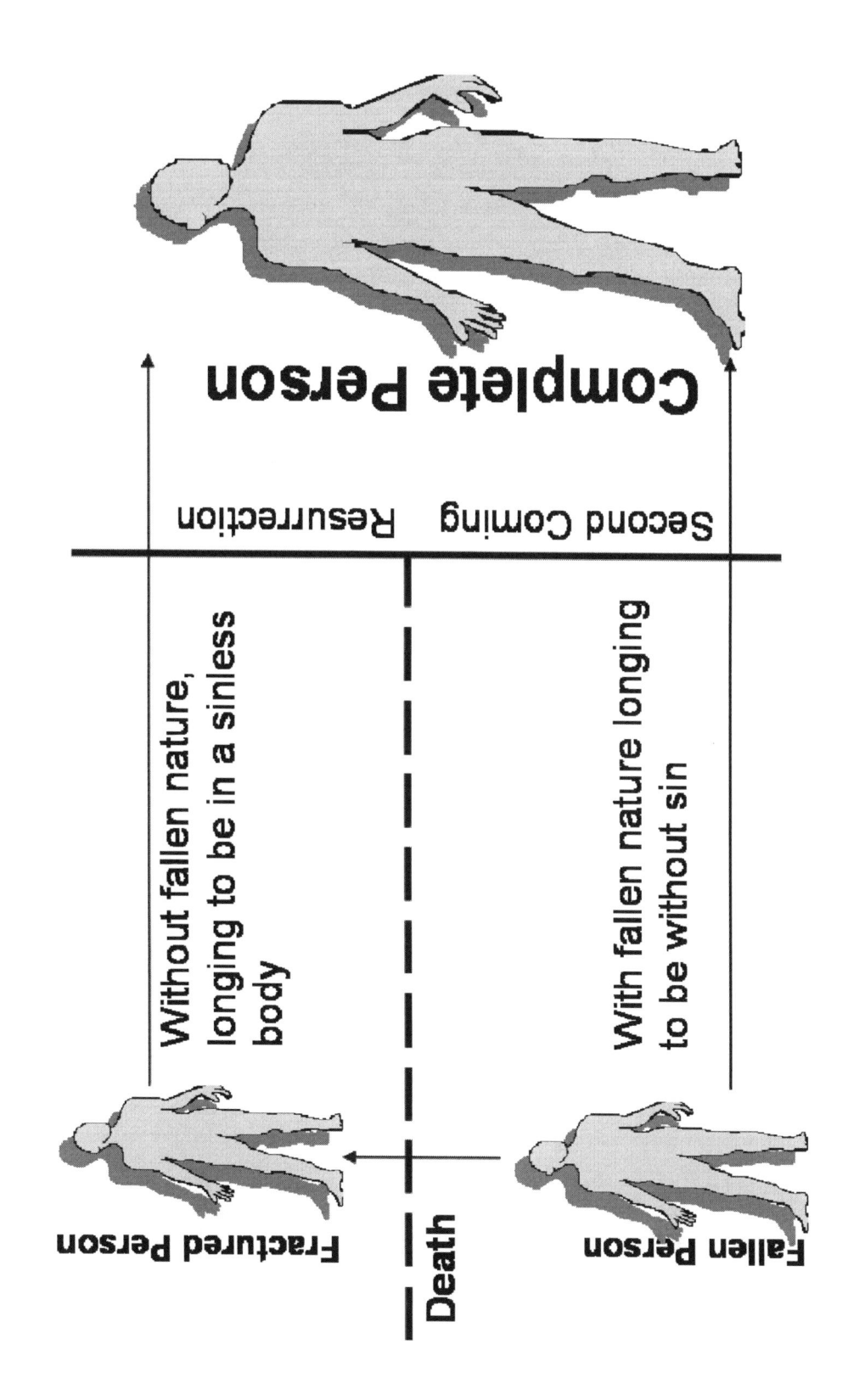

Complete Person

Resurrection | Second Coming

Without fallen nature, longing to be in a sinless body

With fallen nature longing to be without sin

Fractured Person

Death

Fallen Person

Defense of Conditional Unity:

1. Arguments made in favor of dichotomy are compelling because they point to an intermediate state. This is when the immaterial part of man will exist without the body. Therefore, Conditional Unity is in full agreement with the views of dichotomy. However, the separation made at death between the material and immaterial is an unnatural separation in which people will long to be united with their body because the body is an essential part of humanity.

2 Corinthians 5:4
"Our dying bodies make us groan and sigh, but it's not that we want to die and have no bodies at all. We want to slip into our new bodies so that these dying bodies will be swallowed up by everlasting life."

1 Corinthians 15:53–54
"For this perishable body must put on the imperishable, and this mortal body must put on immortality. Now when this perishable puts on the imperishable, and this mortal puts on immortality, then the saying that is written will happen, 'Death has been swallowed up in victory.'"

2. The unredeemed will be judged as whole persons (material and immaterial), since they also will take part in the resurrection. This suggests that the body is an integral part of humanity, so much so that judgment cannot proceed without it.

Daniel 12:2
"Many of those who sleep in the dust of the ground will awake, these to everlasting life, but the others to disgrace and everlasting contempt."

John 5:28–29
"Do not marvel at this; for an hour is coming, in which all who are in the tombs will hear His voice, and will come forth; those who did the good deeds to a resurrection of life, those who committed the evil deeds to a resurrection of judgment."

SESSION 3: THE CONSTITUTION OF MAN: DUALISM

3. Monistic arguments that place the emphasis of our hope in the resurrection are compelling because both the New Testament and the Old place much emphasis in the resurrection and the coming kingdom, not in any intermediate state of existence or in heaven.

1 Thessalonians 4:13
"But we do not want you to be uninformed, brethren, about those who are asleep, so that you will not grieve as do the rest who have no hope. For if we believe that Jesus died and rose again, even so God will bring with Him those who have fallen asleep in Jesus. For this we say to you by the word of the Lord, that we who are alive and remain until the coming of the Lord, will not precede those who have fallen asleep. For the Lord Himself will descend from heaven with a shout, with the voice of the archangel and with the trumpet of God, and the dead in Christ will rise first. Then we who are alive and remain will be caught up together with them in the clouds to meet the Lord in the air, and so we shall always be with the Lord. Therefore comfort one another with these words."

Matthew 6:9–10
"Pray, then, in this way: 'Our Father who is in heaven, hallowed be Your name. Your kingdom come. Your will be done, on earth as it is in heaven.'"

Positive Implications of Conditional Unity:

1. The Bible speaks of a unified self in terms of both judgment and redemption.

2. When man fell, he fell as a whole person.

3. When man is redeemed, he is redeemed as a whole person.

4. Our physical condition is intricately linked to that of our soul/spirit. When our soul/spirit is troubled, it has direct and immediate effects on our body.

5. The condition of our soul is intricately linked to our physical condition. When we are unhealthy, fail to get proper exercise, or are chemically depressed, our spirit/soul suffers.

Monism ⟶ Body/Brain =

Trichotomy
Dichotomy ⟶ Body/Brain ≠
Conditional Unity

What is Gnostic Dualism?

Gnostic Dualism: Man's constitution is physical and spiritual. The physical body is a burdensome, temporary and material confinement out of which we long to escape.

Adherents: Many uninformed Christians who have not taken Humanity and Sin through TTP.

SESSION 3: THE CONSTITUTION OF MAN: DUALISM

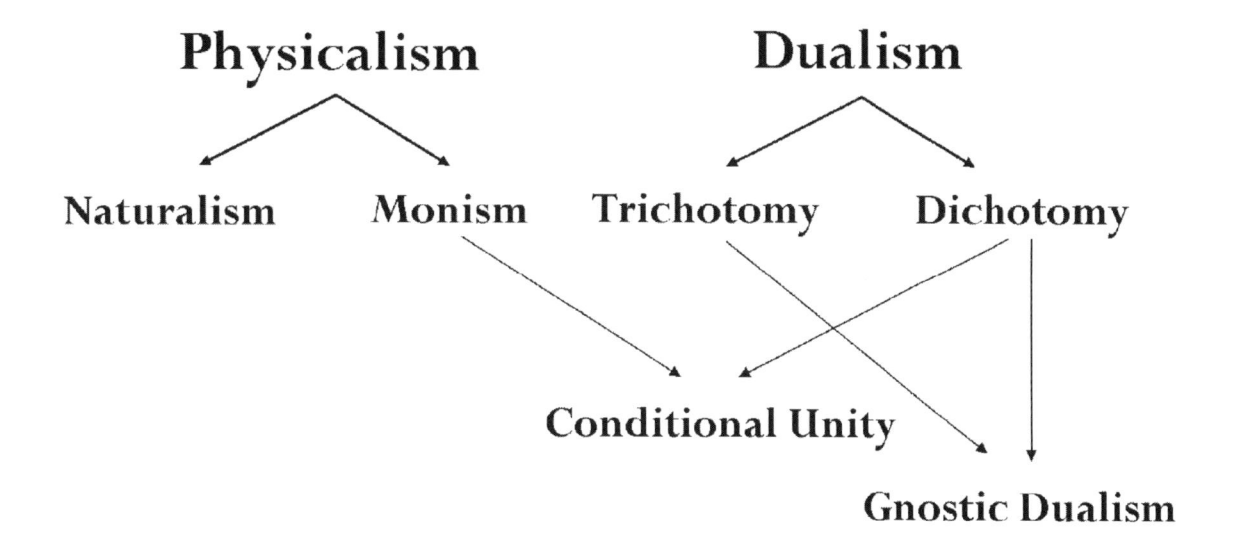

```
Physicalism              Dualism
  /      \              /       \
Naturalism  Monism   Trichotomy  Dichotomy

         Conditional Unity

              Gnostic Dualism
```

Negative Effects:

1. Produces in some cases an unbalanced view on what it means to be human.

2. Creates a negative view on physical pleasures that God gave man as gifts (sex, food, etc.).

3. Causes people to believe that this life does not really matter.

4. Devalues the physical by placing it secondary to the spiritual.

5. Disillusions people about the nature of their eternal existence.

SESSION 3: THE CONSTITUTION OF MAN: DUALISM

GROUP DISCUSSION QUESTIONS

1. One argument for Dualism is that it is a common belief among people of all cultures and civilizations that they are more than just a body. Most believe the "I" or the "me" transcends the physical. Do you feel this way? Please explain. Discuss the values and problems with this type of argument.

2. Dualism teaches that people are more than just a body. How has your own personal experience confirmed or denied this doctrine.

3. Read the story of the Rich man and Lazarus. Does this parable support Monism or Dualism? Please explain.

How might a Monist respond to this parable?

4. Which of the three positions, (Dichotomy, Trichotomy, Conditional Unity) most persuades you? Please explain why.

5. When you are physically sick, how is your spiritual life affected?

6. Read Psalm 32:1-4. When you are spiritually sick, how is your physical life affected? Give personal examples.

7. Review Gnostic Dualism. In what ways do you see the influence of Gnostic Dualism in society?

8. In what ways do you see the influence of Gnostic Dualism in your own personal life? How can you change this?

9. How is your thinking most challenged by the lesson? Please explain.

Session 4

CREATION OF THE SOUL
When and how was the soul created?

Questions:

- When was the soul created?
- What part, if any, do our parents play in the creation of the soul?
- Is the soul "inserted" into our body? If so, when? At conception? After conception? At birth? Or sometime after birth?
- Does it really matter?

Psalm 139:1-17

"O LORD, you examine me and know. 2 You know when I sit down and when I get up; even from far away you understand my motives. 3 You carefully observe me when I travel or when I lie down to rest; you are aware of everything I do. 4 Certainly my tongue does not frame a word without you, O LORD, being thoroughly aware of it. 5 You squeeze me in from behind and in front; you place your hand on me. 6 Your knowledge is beyond my comprehension; it is so far beyond me, I am unable to fathom it. 7 Where can I go to escape your spirit? Where can I flee to escape your presence? 8 If I were to ascend to heaven, you would be there. If I were to sprawl out in Sheol, there you would be. 9 If I were to fly away on the wings of the dawn, and settle down on the other side of the sea, 10 even there your hand would guide me, your right hand would grab hold of me. 11 If I were to say, 'Certainly the darkness will cover me, and the light will turn to night all around me,' 12 even the darkness is not too dark for you to see, and the night is as bright as day; darkness and light are the same to you. 13 Certainly you made my mind and heart; you wove me together in my mother's womb. 14 I will give you thanks because your deeds are awesome and amazing. You knew me thoroughly; 15 my bones were not hidden from you, when I was made in secret and sewed together in the depths of the earth. 16 Your eyes saw me when I was inside the womb. All the days ordained for me were recorded in your scroll before one of them came into existence. 17 How difficult it is for me to fathom your thoughts about me, O God! How vast are their sum total!"

Options:

1. Pre-existence Theory
2. Creation Theory
3. Traducian Theory

Pre-existence Theory:

This theory teaches that people's souls/spirits are eternal and, therefore, preexist the creation of their bodies. The sin nature can be attributed to the former state of existence in which the person sinned.

Adherents: Origen, Delitzsch

Creation Theory:

This theory is that God Himself creates each person's soul individually, and then places the soul in the body.

Adherents: Grudem, Hodge, Berkhof, Calvin, and Roman Catholics

Traducian Theory:

Comes from the Latin tradux, meaning "inheritance, transmission." This theory teaches that the soul is created in and with the body by the parents. While God is the ultimate creator of all things, he uses people intermediately or as secondary causes.

Adherents: Tertullian, Luther, and Jonathan Edwards

What say you?

SESSION 4: CREATION OF THE SOUL

Arguments for Pre-existence Theory:

1. No biblical or philosophical arguments to support this view.

2. Common outcome of Gnostic Dualism.

Arguments for the Creation Theory:

1. The creation account evidences that God creates the body from the earth and the soul is created directly by God.

Genesis 2:7
"And the LORD God formed man of the dust of the ground, and breathed into his nostrils the breath of life; and man became a living soul." (KJV)

2. The Bible explicitly says that God created the soul.

Zechariah 12:1
"The revelation of the word of the LORD concerning Israel: The LORD—He who stretches out the heavens and lays the foundations of the earth, who forms the human spirit within a person—says."

Hebrews 12:9
"Besides, we have experienced discipline from our earthly fathers and we respected them; shall we not submit ourselves all the more to the Father of spirits and receive life?"

3. Christ was like us in every way, yet without sin. If God does not create each soul individually, Christ's soul was not created by God, but by Mary (since He is like us in every way). If this is the case, Christ's soul is sinful like hers.

Response to Creation Theory:

1.	This evidences a bad translation in the KJV. The creation account speaks not to the creation of the soul, but the giving of life as most modern translations recognize. The same is said of the animals when God gives them life.

Genesis 2:7
"The LORD God formed the man from the soil of the ground and breathed into his nostrils the breath of life, and the man became a living being." (emphasis added. NET; also see NIV, ESV, NLT, NAS)

Genesis 1:30
"'And to all the animals of the earth, and to every bird of the air, and to all the creatures that move on the ground—everything that has the breath of life [nephash] in it—I give every green plant for food.' It was so."

2.	This is trying to say too much about the direct creation of the soul. God is the ultimate Creator of all things, material and immaterial, but this does not mean that He does not use intermediaries in the creation process. If this argument were true, then it would also have to mean that God directly created the body without using the parents as the intermediate cause since Ps. 139:13-15 says that God formed our body.

Psalm 136:13-15
"Certainly you made my mind and heart; you wove me together in my mother's womb. I will give you thanks because your deeds are awesome and amazing. You knew me thoroughly; my bones were not hidden from you, when I was made in secret and sewed together in the depths of the earth."

3. It could be that Christ did not have original sin because it is inherited through the Father. This would explain the necessity of the virgin birth.

SESSION 4: CREATION OF THE SOUL

Arguments for Traducian Theory:

1. It better explains the inheritance of original sin and corruption as being handed down, in both body and soul, by Adam.

On the other hand, if God creates each soul directly, and each person is born sinful in both body and soul, then how did the soul become sinful? Did God create a sinful soul and then unite it to the sin corrupted body? This would make God the author of sin—not man.

2. There is no problem in saying that people have been granted the power to create a soul as well as a body. To object would devalue the miraculous nature of the creation of the body.

On the other hand, to say that God must create the soul directly because man does have such great power of creativity, evidences a Gnostic understanding of the separation between the body and the soul, believing that the soul is more important, virtuous, or miraculous than the body.

Positive Implications of the Traducian Theory:

1. It does not give undue prominence to the soul by saying it is the only part of the human constitution that is created directly by God.

2. It fits better with the Conditional Unity theory of man.

3. It fits better with the understanding of original sin in that there remains a complete solidarity of the human race.

4. There is no doubt that man is a complete and whole person at the time of conception.

If God did not indirectly create man's soul/spirit through the parents, but directly created it Himself, how can we be sure when He gives the soul to a person? In other words, how do we know when a "fetus" (body) becomes a person (body and soul/spirit)?

    – At conception?   – Sometime after?
    – At the age of accountability?   – At birth?

GROUP DISCUSSION QUESTIONS

1. Many people would see this lesson as irrelevant to real life and therefore not important. Do you think the study of the creation of the soul is relevant?

Please explain.

2. The pre-existence theory says that our souls pre-existed the creation of our body. How have you seen this view implicitly evidenced by people's beliefs?

3. The creation view of the soul has been popular throughout church history. Why do you think that this view is attractive?

4. The traducian view of the soul says that parents are intermediate causes for the creation of the soul. Do you think that it is possible for this to be the case? Please explain why or why not.

SESSION 4: CREATION OF THE SOUL

5. Do you think that it is possible to be a creationist and to support abortion. Keep in mind that, according to the creationist view, we cannot be absolutely certain when God joins the soul with the body? Why or why not?

6. The study of the creation of the soul has become somewhat of a theological pastime. Most people have never dealt with the issues presented in this lesson.

Why do you think this is the case?

7. How is your thinking most challenged by this lesson? Please explain.

Session 5

THE *IMAGO DEI* IN HUMANITY

What does it mean that we are in the image of God?

Questions:

- Do humans carry dignity as God's image bearers?
- Do humans alone carry the image of God? What about animals? Do they have the image of God?
- What affect did the fall have on the image of God? Did humanity lose this image after the Fall?
- How should the fact that man is created in the image of God affect the way we treat one another?

Imago Dei :   (Lat. "image of God"). Refers to the fact that humanity carries a unique resemblance to God.

Genesis 1:26-27
"Then God said, 'Let Us make man in Our image, according to Our likeness; and let them rule over the fish of the sea and over the birds of the sky and over the cattle and over all the earth, and over every creeping thing that creeps on the earth.' God created man in His own image, in the image of God He created him; male and female He created them."

Psalm 8:3-8
"When I consider Your heavens, the work of Your fingers, the moon and the stars, which You have ordained; what is man that You take thought of him, and the son of man that You care for him? Yet You have made him a little lower than God, And You crown him with glory and majesty! You make him to rule over the works of Your hands; You have put all things under his feet, all sheep and oxen, and also the beasts of the field, the birds of the heavens and the fish of the sea, whatever passes through the paths of the seas."

What do these verses tell us about the meaning of being created in the image of God?

What else does it mean to be created in God's image?

Aspects of the Imago Dei

	God	Man	Animal
Personality	Yes	Yes	
Eternality	Yes	Yes	
Relationality	Yes	Yes	
Volitionality	Yes	Yes	
Rationality	Yes	Yes	
Spirituality	Yes	Yes	
Physicality	No	Yes	
Morality	Yes	Yes	
Dominionality	Yes	Yes	

SESSION 5: THE IMAGO DEI IN HUMANITY

> "I would infer that everything we are reflects God in some way, though everything we are is also different from God!"
>
> —John Frame
>
> _{John Piper and Wayne Grudem, ed., *Recovering Biblical Manhood and Womanhood* (Wheaton, IL: Crossway, 1991).}

> "These differences between human beings and the rest of creation are not *absolute differences* but often differences of very great degree. . . . The more complex and highly developed animals are *more* like God than lower forms of animals. Therefore, we should not say that *only* man reflects any likeness to God at all, for in one way or another all of creation reflects some likeness to God. But it is still important to recognize that *only* man, out of all creation, is so like God that he can be said to be "in the image of God." . . . In some respect the differences are absolute, and in other respects they are relative, but they are significant."
>
> —Wayne Grudem
>
> _{Wayne Grudem, *Systematic Theology* (Grand Rapids, MI: IVP, 1994), 449.}

Personality: Like God, people are individual beings with self consciousness.

Eternality: Like God, people will exist into eternity.

Relationality: Like God, people have a capacity and drive for relationships.

Volitionality:	Like God, people have the freedom and ability to make volitional choices according to their will.
Rationality:	Like God, people have the ability to think, contemplate, and reflect on abstract ideas, future plans, and past events, advancing toward a more beneficial existence through problem solving.
Spirituality:	Like God, people are spiritual beings possessing an immaterial part of their constitution.
Physicality:	Unlike God, people have a material part of their constitution that is corporeal. But like God, people have senses that come as a direct result of our physicality, such as man's ability to see and to hear.
Morality:	Like God, people are inherently moral creatures, understanding that there is good and evil (although this was gained as a result of the Fall).
Dominionality:	Like God, people have been given authority to rule over creation, using all its resources for their benefit, enjoyment, and survival.

How did the fall affect the Imago Dei?

Options:

1. Man fully retains the imago Dei and only misrepresents it through personal sin.
2. Man fully lost the imago Dei. It is restored only in Christ.
3. The imago Dei has been retained in all men, but marred by sin. It is restored in Christ

SESSION 5: THE IMAGO DEI IN HUMANITY

Scripture clearly states that the imago Dei has been retained to some degree in all people:

Genesis 5:1-3
"This is the book of the generations of Adam. In the day when God created man, He made him in the likeness of God. He created them male and female, and He blessed them and named them Man in the day when they were created. When Adam had lived one hundred and thirty years, he became the father of a son in his own likeness, according to his image, and named him Seth."

Genesis 9:6
"Whoever sheds man's blood, by man his blood shall be shed, because in the image of God He made man."

James 3:8-9
"But no one can tame the tongue; it is a restless evil and full of deadly poison. With it we bless our Lord and Father, and with it we curse men, who have been made in the likeness of God."

Fill out this chart:

	Fully retained	Distorted	Fully lost
Personality			
Eternality			
Relationality			
Volitionality			
Rationality			
Spirituality			
Physicality			
Morality			
Dominionality			

GROUP DISCUSSION QUESTIONS

1. In what ways does our society measure the dignity of a person? Is this biblical?

2. In what ways do you "follow the crowd" in using the wrong criteria to measure the dignity of man? How can you correct this?

3. Do you really believe that all people have dignity as image bearers of God?

What often makes you question whether this is true?

4. In what ways do you see unbelievers reflect the image of God more than believers? Please explain.

SESSION 5: THE IMAGO DEI IN HUMANITY

5. How do Christians often have an unbalanced pessimism about man? Give examples.

6. How do Christians often have an unbalanced optimism about man? Give examples.

7. In what ways do we treat others (believers and non-believers) with less dignity than they deserve, being created in God's image? Give examples.

8. How should the knowledge that all people are created in the image of God affect ministry? (For example: teaching and evangelism).

9. How was your thinking challenged the most by the lesson? Please explain.

Session 6

ORIGINAL SIN: PELAGIANISM
How far did we fall?

Outline for the Fall of Man

    A. Original Sin
    B. Free Will?

Questions:

- Is man good at heart?
- Is it possible for man to live without sin?
- How did Adam's sin affect mankind?
- Does God hold a person guilty for the sin of another?

What is Original Sin?

> "I wasn't jumping, for me it was a fall, it's a long way down to nothing at all."
>
> —Bono, "Stuck in a Moment"

The Prohibition:
Read Genesis 2:8-9, 15-16

The Violation:
Read Genesis 3:1-6

The Penalty:
Read Genesis 3:7-24

Key Terms

Original Sin: A broad term that refers to the effects that the first sin had on humanity or to the "origin" of sin.

Imputed Sin: Specifically refers to the guilt or condemnation of the first sin which was imputed to humanity. (Also: original guilt)

Inherited Sin: Specifically refers to the transferal of the sinful nature. (Also: original corruption, original pollution, sinful nature)

Personal Sin: Specifically refers to the sins that are committed by individuals.

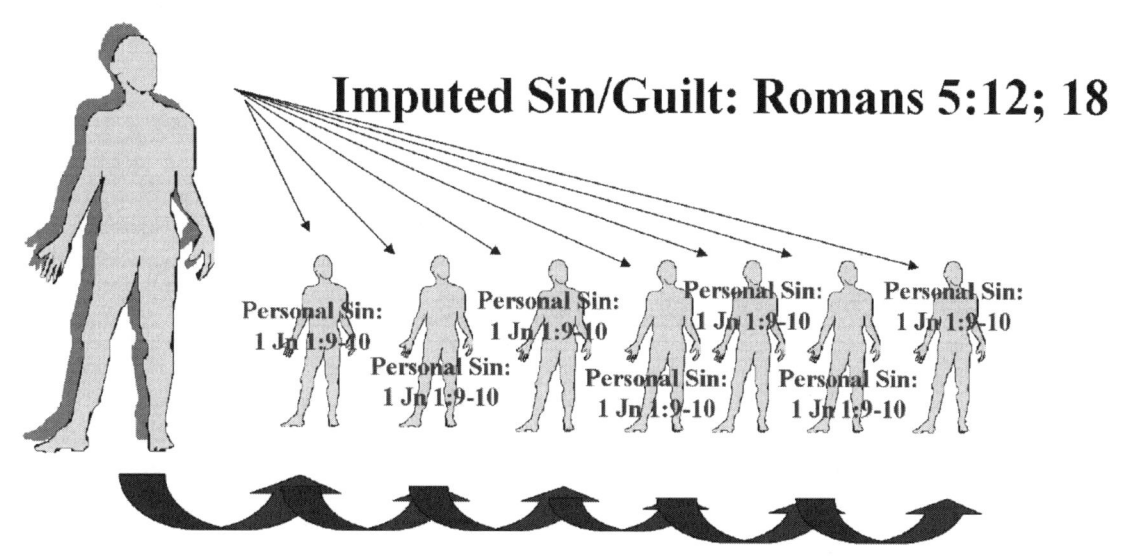

SESSION 6: ORIGINAL SIN: PELAGIANISM

Imputed Sin/Guilt: Romans 5:12; 18

Personal Sin: 1 Jn 1:9-10 *(repeated for multiple figures)*

Inherited Corruption: Psalm 51:5

Original Sin

> "What is at stake? The importance of the doctrine of original sin cannot be overstated. Doctrinally speaking, this doctrine has split the Church in two for centuries. It is the starting point for one's view of salvation. How one views the condition of humanity will affect how they view the necessity of the grace of God. A denial of the corruption brought by original sin would, in effect, deny the inherent need for man's redemption. On the other hand, a denial of man's responsibility before God would, in effect, deny the justice in condemning a person since they would be blamed for something they did not actually do."
>
> —Rhome Dyck and Michael Patton

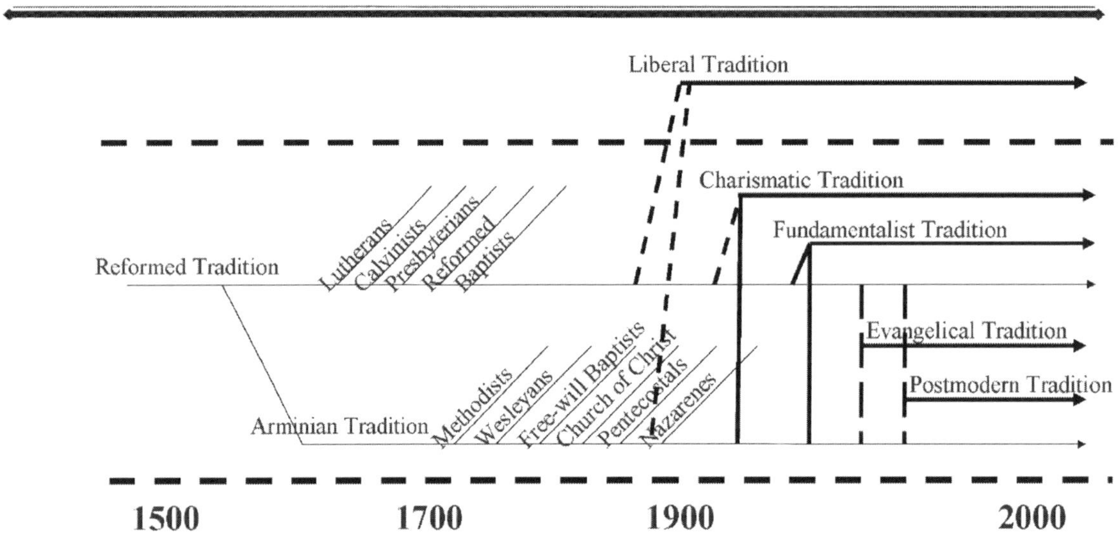
Liberal Tradition
Charismatic Tradition
Fundamentalist Tradition
Reformed Tradition
Lutherans
Calvinists
Presbyterians
Reformed
Baptists
Evangelical Tradition
Postmodern Tradition
Arminian Tradition
Methodists
Wesleyans
Free-will Baptists
Church of Christ
Pentecostals
Nazarenes
1500
1700
1900
2000

Three views:

1. Pelagianism
2. Augustinianism
3. Arminianism

How did the fall affect our will?

SESSION 6: ORIGINAL SIN: PELAGIANISM

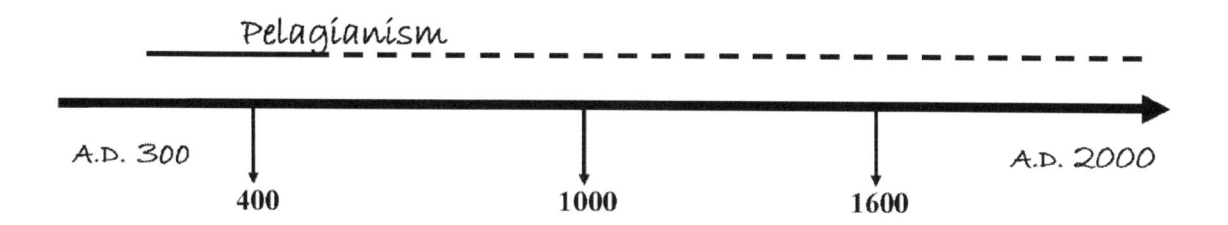

Pelagianism ———— (A.D. 300 — 400 — 1000 — 1600 — A.D. 2000)

Pelagianism: Man is inherently good. The Fall did not bring condemnation upon any but Adam. As well, the disposition of the will is unaffected. Man is born like Adam with the same ability to choose between good and evil. Man sins as a result of bad examples that began with Adam.

Proponent: Pelagius (ca.350-418), British monk.

Adherents: Liberal Christianity, Socinians.

Condemned: Council of Orange.

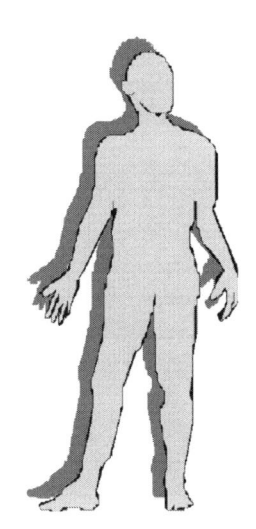

Personal Sin: 1 Jn 1:9-10
Personal Sin: 1 Jn 1:9-10
Personal Sin: 1 Jn 1:9-10
Personal Sin: 1 Jn 1:9-10
Personal Sin: 1 Jn 1:9-10
Personal Sin: 1 Jn 1:9-10
Personal Sin: 1 Jn 1:9-10

Defense of Pelagianism:

1. God does not hold people accountable for the sins of another.

> **Jeremiah 31:29-30**
> "In those days they will not say again, 'The fathers have eaten sour grapes, and the children's teeth are set on edge.' But everyone will die for his own iniquity; each man who eats the sour grapes, his teeth will be set on edge."

> **Ezekiel 18:19-20**
> "Yet you say, 'Why should the son not bear the punishment for the father's iniquity?' When the son has practiced justice and righteousness and has observed all My statutes and done them, he shall surely live. The person who sins will die. The son will not bear the punishment for the father's iniquity, nor will the father bear the punishment for the son's iniquity; the righteousness of the righteous will be upon himself, and the wickedness of the wicked will be upon himself."

2. If sinful corruption is passed on to all people from Adam, then people have an inherent disposition which denies that they have TRUE freedom. Why would God then command and expect people to do things that cannot be done? The Bible clearly illustrates that man has a free will that can choose good or evil with no inherent disposition to either.

Read Deuteronomy 30:15-20

Evil   Good

Condition of the will

SESSION 6: ORIGINAL SIN: PELAGIANISM

GROUP DISCUSSION QUESTIONS

1. Pelagius believed that people are born with a neutral will. In other words, people are unaffected by the fall of Adam and only do wrong as a result of bad influences. How have you seen this view evidenced in society?

2. Do you believe that people do wrong as a result of bad influences?

3. Do you agree that people are born neutral? Why or why not?

4. It has been said that all people are born Pelagian until they are told otherwise. Do you agree?

Please explain.

5. Do you agree with the Pelagian view that man did not inherit the sin of Adam? If not, how do you reconcile your view with this verse?

> **Ezekiel 18:19-20**
> "Yet you say, 'Why should the son not bear the punishment for the father's iniquity?' When the son has practiced justice and righteousness and has observed all My statutes and done them, he shall surely live. The person who sins will die. The son will not bear the punishment for the father's iniquity, nor will the father bear the punishment for the son's iniquity; the righteousness of the righteous will be upon himself, and the wickedness of the wicked will be upon himself."

6. How was your thinking most challenged by the lesson? Please explain.

Session 7

ORIGINAL SIN: AUGUSTINIANISM & ARMINIANISM

How far did we fall?

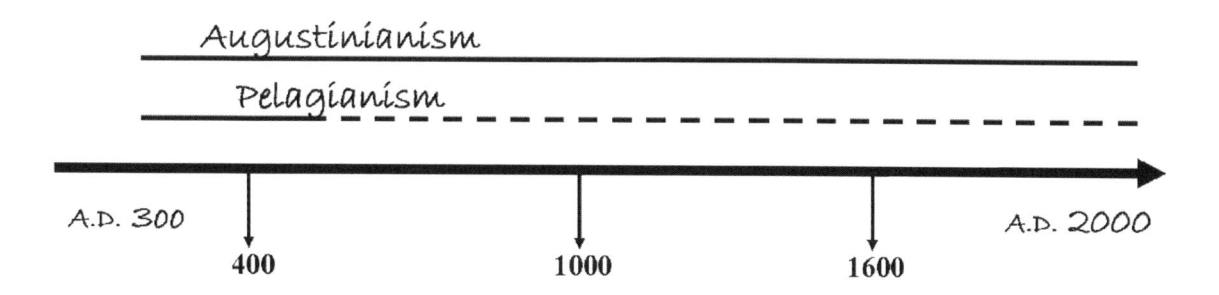

```
    Augustinianism
    ─────────────────────────────────────────────
      Pelagianism
      ──────────────── ─ ─ ─ ─ ─ ─ ─ ─ ─ ─ ─ ─ ─

━━━━━━━━━━━━━━━━━━━━━━━━━━━━━━━━━━━━━━━━━━━━━━━━━▶
  A.D. 300     ↓              ↓              ↓          A.D. 2000
              400            1000           1600
```

Augustinianism: Man is inherently corrupt. The Fall brought condemnation and guilt upon all men. As well, the disposition of the will is totally corrupted and inclined toward evil. Man has free will, but that will is governed by his sinful nature. Man sins, therefore, because he is a sinner.

Proponent: Augustine (354-430), bishop of Hippo.

Adherents: Gregory, Anselm, Luther, Gregory, Anselm, Luther, Calvin, Jonathan Edwards, R.C. Sproul, Charles Ryrie.

Imputed Sin/Guilt: Romans 5:12; 18

Personal Sin: 1 Jn 1:9-10

Inherited Corruption: Psalm 51:5

Westminster Confession of Faith
Chapter VI: Of the Fall of Man, of Sin, and the Punishment Thereof

I. Our first parents, being seduced by the subtlety and temptations of Satan, sinned in eating the forbidden fruit. This their sin, God was pleased, according to His wise and holy counsel, to permit, having purposed to order it to His own glory.

II. By this sin they fell from their original righteousness and communion, with God, and so became dead in sin, and wholly defiled in all the parts and faculties of soul and body.

III. They being the root of all mankind, the guilt of this sin was imputed; and the same death in sin, and corrupted nature, conveyed to all their posterity descending from them by ordinary generation.

IV. From this original corruption, whereby we are utterly indisposed, disabled, and made opposite to all good, and wholly inclined to all evil, do proceed all actual transgressions

SESSION 7: ORIGINAL SIN: AUGUSTINIANISM & ARMINIANISM

V. This corruption of nature, during this life, does remain in those that are regenerated; and although it be, through Christ, pardoned, and mortified; yet both itself, and all the motions thereof, are truly and properly sin.

VI. Every sin, both original and actual, being a transgression of the righteous law of God, and contrary thereunto, does in its own nature, bring guilt upon the sinner, whereby he is bound over to the wrath of God, and curse of the law, and so made subject to death, with all miseries spiritual, temporal, and eternal.

Defense of Augustinianism:

1. The Bible supports the understanding that we have a corrupt nature that is inherited from our parents in that all people die.

>   **Genesis 2:17**
>   "But from the tree of the knowledge of good and evil you shall not eat, for in the day that you eat from it you will surely die."
>
>   **Hebrews 9:27**
>   "And inasmuch as it is appointed for men to die once and after this comes judgment."

2. The Bible supports the understanding that we have a corrupt nature that is inherited from our parents in that all people are sinners from birth.

>   **Psalm 51:5**
>   "Look, I was prone to do wrong from birth; I was a sinner the moment my mother conceived me."
>
>   **Jeremiah 17:9**
>   "The human mind is more
>
>   **John 3:3**
>   "Jesus answered and said to him, 'Truly, truly, I say to you, unless one is born again he cannot see the kingdom of God.'"

Ephesians 2:1-3
"And you were dead in your trespasses and sins, in which you formerly walked according to the course of this world, according to the prince of the power of the air, of the spirit that is now working in the sons of disobedience. Among them we too all formerly lived in the lusts of our flesh, indulging the desires of the flesh and of the mind, and were by nature children of wrath, even as the rest."

Romans 5:19
"For as through the one man's disobedience the many were made sinners, even so through the obedience of the One the many will be made righteous."

3. If the disposition of the will is unaffected, and there is equal opportunity to choose the good as well as the evil, why is it that all people have sinned? The odds are good, but there never has been a winner.

Romans 3:23
"For all have sinned and fall short of the glory of God."

Genesis 6:5
"Then the LORD saw that the wickedness of man was great on the earth, and that every intent of the thoughts of his heart was only evil continually."

4. The Bible supports the idea that we have inherited Adam's guilt and are condemned before we ever commit a personal sin.

Read Romans 5:12-18

SESSION 7: ORIGINAL SIN: AUGUSTINIANISM & ARMINIANISM

Condition of the will

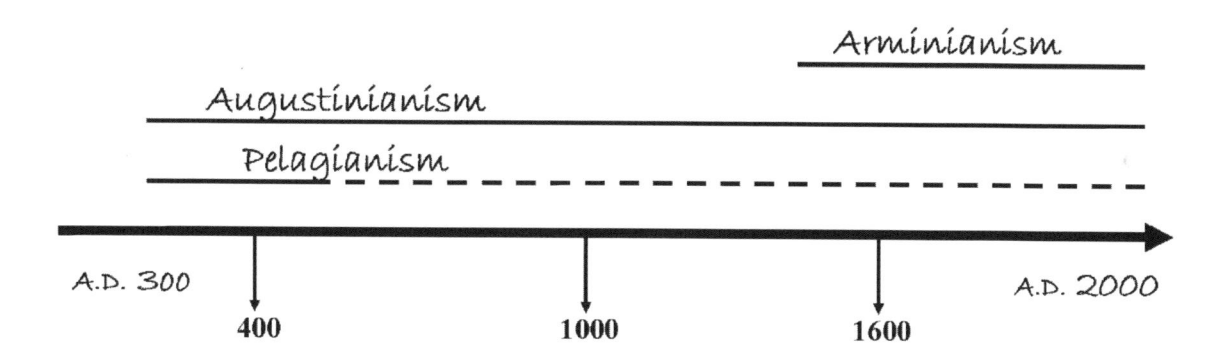

Arminianism

Augustinianism

Pelagianism

A.D. 300 — 400 — 1000 — 1600 — A.D. 2000

Arminianism: Man is inherently corrupt. However, the Fall did not bring condemnation upon any but Adam. Adam's sin is only imputed to us when we commit a personal sin, thereby showing our agreement with Adam. The disposition of the will is corrupted so that mans has an inclination to sin, but God gives man prevenient grace to correct the sinful disposition. Now man is like Adam in the Garden, able to choose good or evil.

Proponent: Arminius (ca.1560-1609)

Adherents: Roman Catholics, Erasmus, Methodists, Church of God, most Pentecostals.

Condemned: Synod of Dort (1618-1619)

Defense of Arminianism:

1. The arguments of Pelagius are compelling in that we cannot be held guilty for the sins of another, and that commands presuppose ability, and ability presupposes freedom.

2. The arguments of Augustine are compelling in that we all have personal sin and corruption. There must be a reason for this.

3. The only way to bring harmony to the two arguments is to state that God must confer sufficient grace upon all men to counteract the effects of the inherited corruption, restoring the will and enabling them to cooperate with God in regeneration.

4. Adam's sin is only imputed to people when they sin in the likeness of Adam.

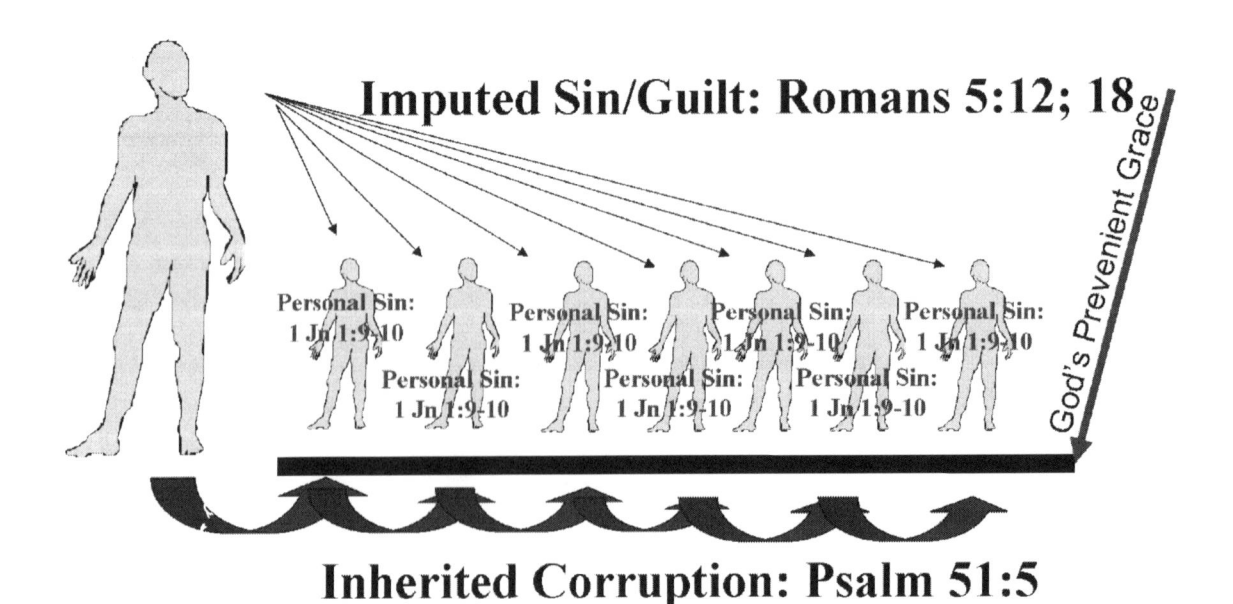

Imputed Sin/Guilt: Romans 5:12; 18

Personal Sin: 1 Jn 1:9-10

God's Prevenient Grace

Inherited Corruption: Psalm 51:5

SESSION 7: ORIGINAL SIN: AUGUSTINIANISM & ARMINIANISM

Condition of the will before prevenient grace

Condition of the will after prevenient grace

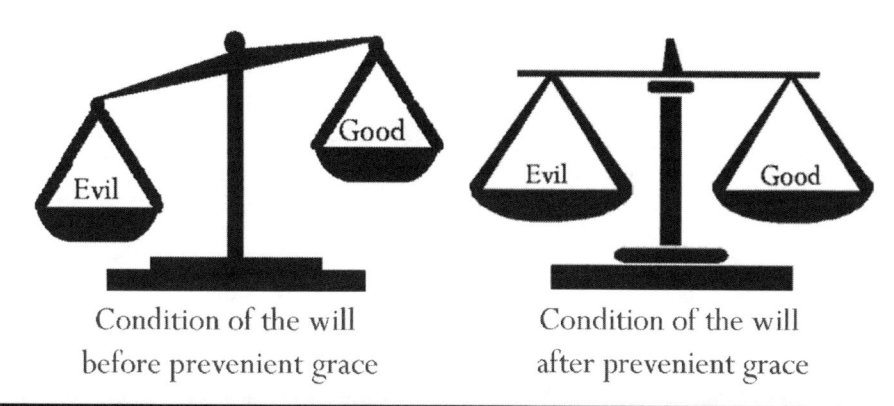

	Relation to Adam's Sin	Relation to Parents' Sin	Free Will
Pelagianism	Bad example	Bad example	Yes
Augustinianism	Imputed sin: Immediate	Inherited sin: Mediated through parents	Yes, but limited by evil nature
Arminianism	Imputed sin: Mediated through our own sin	Inherited sin: Mediated through parents	Yes, restored by prevenient grace

Summary:

A. **Pelagianism:** Man is inherently neutral and able to choose equally between good and evil.

B. **Augustinianism:** Man is inherently evil and unable to choose good without God's sovereign grace.

C. **Arminianism:** Man is corrupted to the degree that God must intervene and provide prevenient (helping) grace so that he might once again be able to choose good.

GROUP DISCUSSION QUESTIONS

1. Augustinianism was accepted by the early church as the council of Orange, while Pelagianism was condemned. While this was not an official ecclesiastical council, it has been a reference for orthodoxy for about 1500 years. Why do you think that the church was so emphatic in its condemnation of Pelagianism and in favor of Augustinianism?

2. Arminianism relies upon the concept of prevenient grace. Prevenient grace, according to Arminianism, has a neutralizing effect upon the will. So while all people were born sinners, unable to choose God on their own, God, at some point in their lives, intervenes with prevenient grace, giving them the ability to choose Him. Evaluate the Arminian doctrine of prevenient grace.

3. Augustinianism believes that all mankind fell with Adam to such a degree that they are completely unable to choose God without God choosing them. Evaluate the Augustinian doctrine of the fall.

SESSION 7: ORIGINAL SIN: AUGUSTINIANISM & ARMINIANISM

4. Having seen and considered all the various positions with regards to our relationship with Adam, which view do you find the most compelling?

Why?

5. How was your thinking most challenged by the lesson? Please explain.

Session 8

FREE WILL
Do we really have a free will?

Define free will.

Three Positions:

Fatalism: Belief that a person's life and choices are totally and unalterably the result of an endless series of cause and effect.

Compatibilism: Belief that a person's actions are free and are determined by their own character and desires.

Libertarianism: Belief that a person's actions are uncaused by any coercion whatsoever (also known as indeterminalism). The agent is the "first cause" of the effect of his or her action.

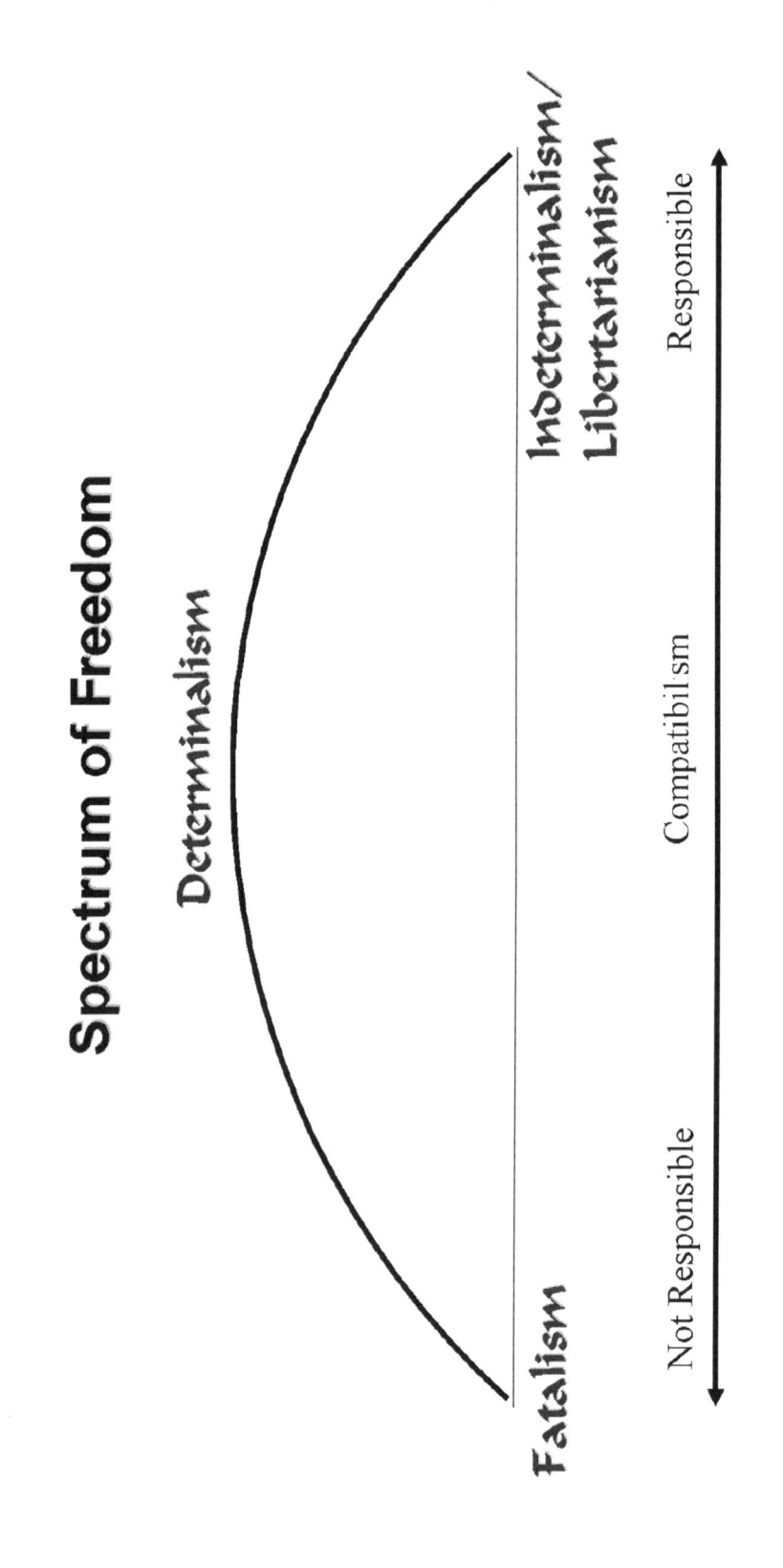

Spectrum of Freedom

Determinism

Indeterminism/ Libertarianism

Fatalism

Not Responsible ← Compatibilism → Responsible

Naturalistic

↓

Fatalism

Theistic

↙ ↘

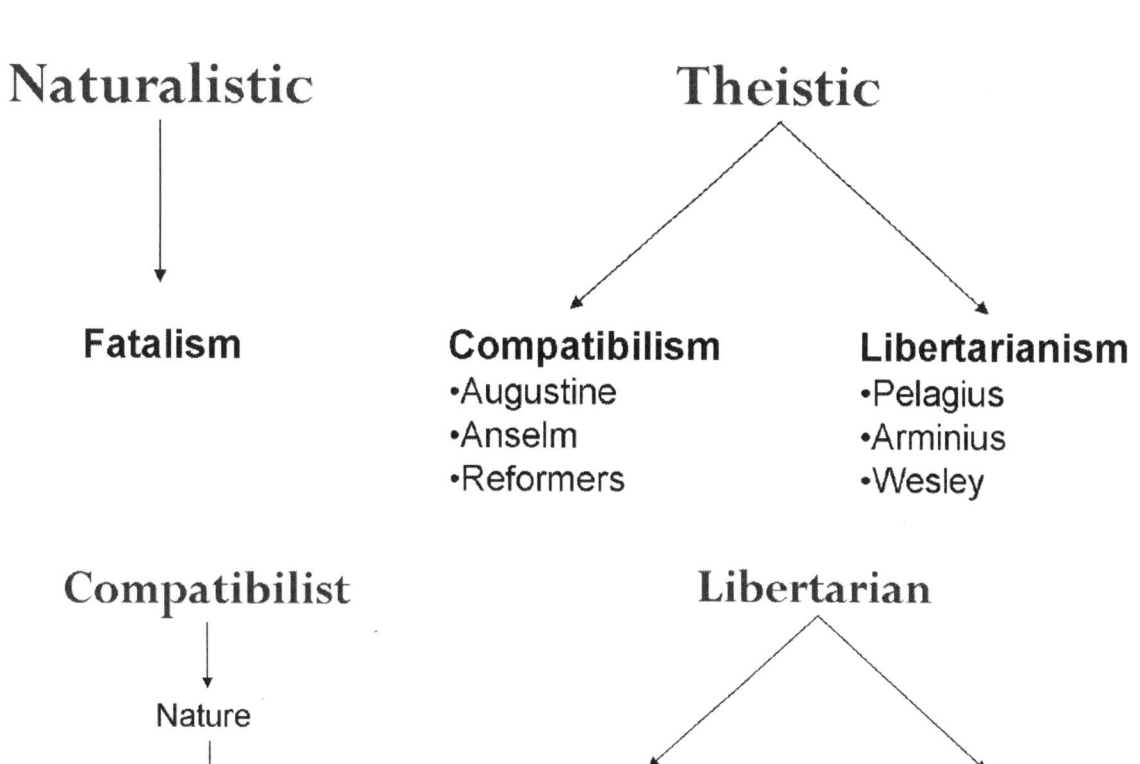

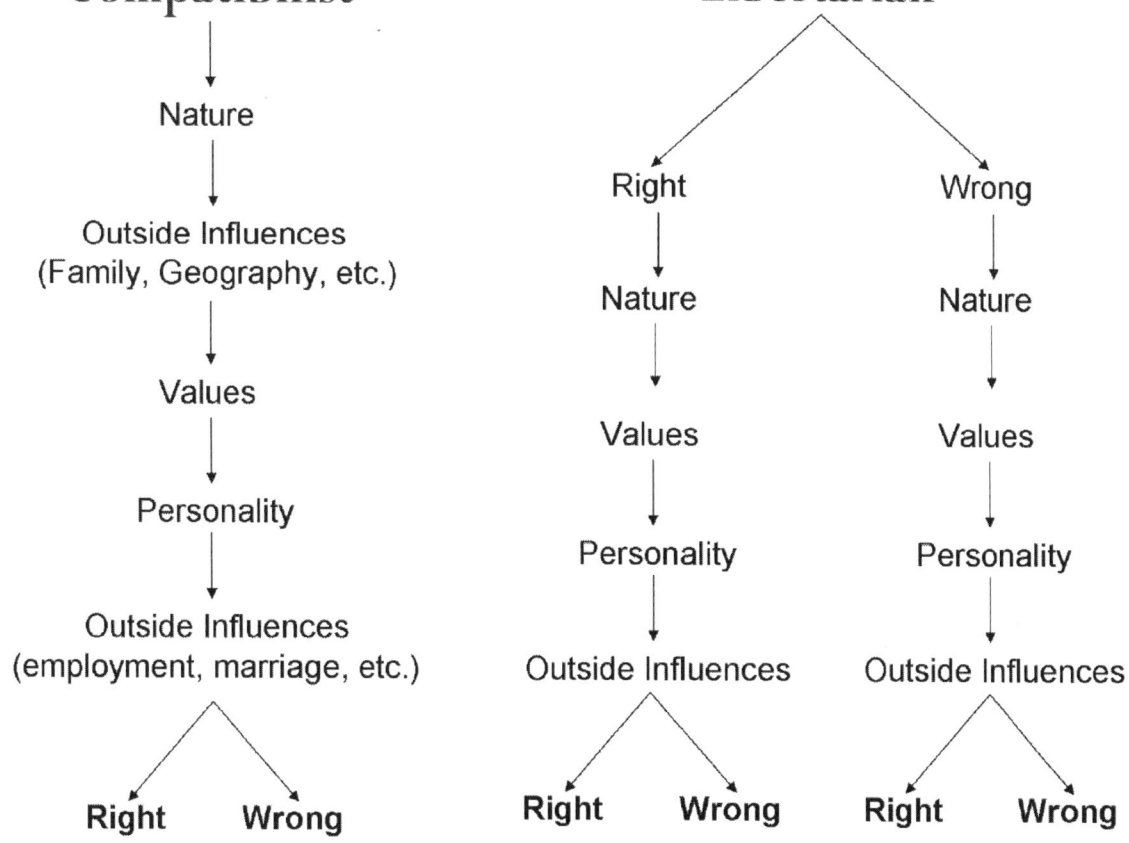

Compatibilism
- Augustine
- Anselm
- Reformers

Libertarianism
- Pelagius
- Arminius
- Wesley

Compatibilist

↓

Nature

↓

Outside Influences
(Family, Geography, etc.)

↓

Values

↓

Personality

↓

Outside Influences
(employment, marriage, etc.)

↙ ↘

Right **Wrong**

Libertarian

↙ ↘

Right → Nature → Values → Personality → Outside Influences → **Right** / **Wrong**

Wrong → Nature → Values → Personality → Outside Influences → **Right** / **Wrong**

Compatibilist: Natural Man

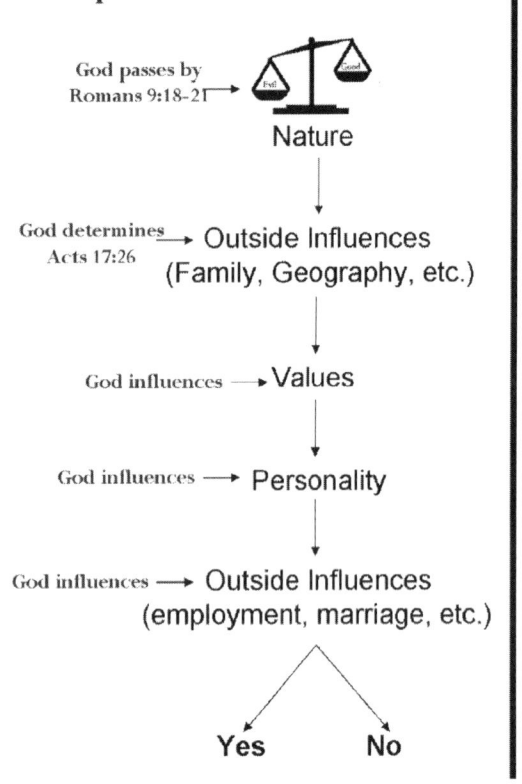

God passes by
Romans 9:18-21 → [scales: Evil/Good]
Nature
↓
God determines → Outside Influences
Acts 17:26 (Family, Geography, etc.)
↓
God influences → Values
↓
God influences → Personality
↓
God influences → Outside Influences
(employment, marriage, etc.)
↓
Yes   No

Compatibilist: Regenerate Man

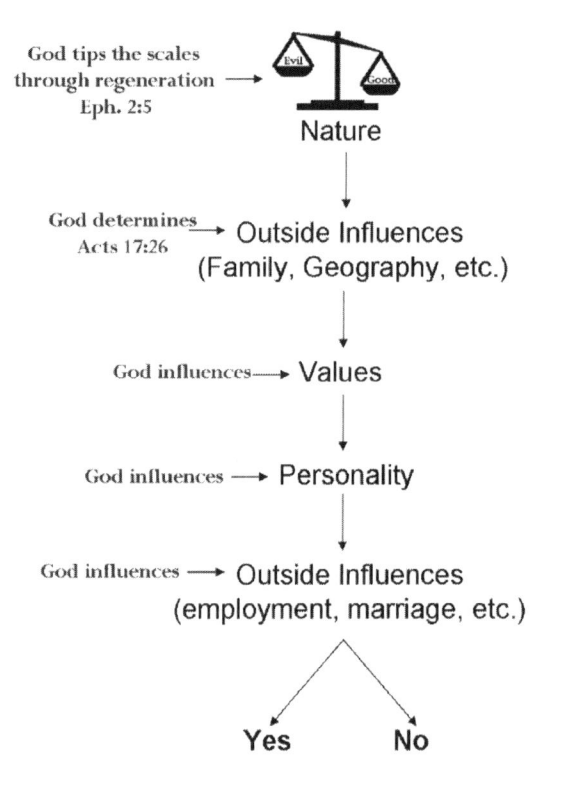

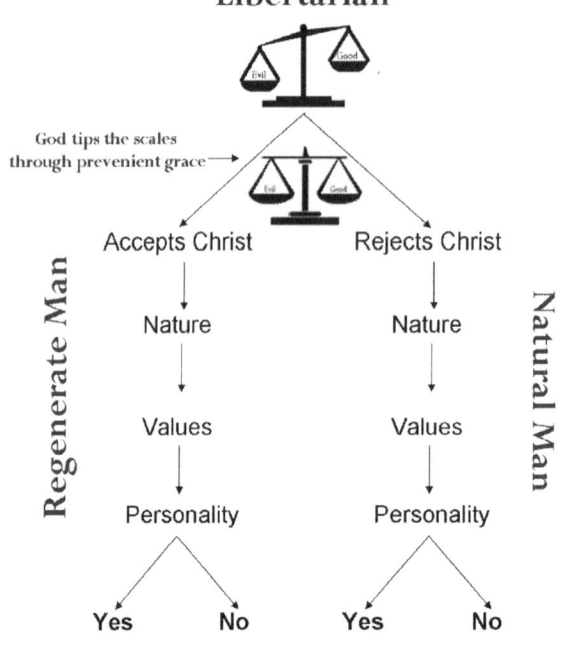

God tips the scales
through regeneration → [scales: Evil/Good]
Eph. 2:5
Nature
↓
God determines → Outside Influences
Acts 17:26 (Family, Geography, etc.)
↓
God influences → Values
↓
God influences → Personality
↓
God influences → Outside Influences
(employment, marriage, etc.)
↓
Yes   No

Libertarian

[scales: Evil/Good]
↓
God tips the scales
through prevenient grace → [scales: Evil/Good]
↙   ↘
Accepts Christ   Rejects Christ
↓   ↓
Nature   Nature
↓   ↓
Values   Values
↓   ↓
Personality   Personality
↙   ↘   ↙   ↘
Yes   No   Yes   No

Regenerate Man   Natural Man

Problems with Compatibilism:

1. Difficult to see how a person's acts can be both free and determined.

2. Why would God still find fault in man if he is the first cause that placed him in the circumstances that have determined his choices?

Problems with Libertarianism:

1. As nice as it sounds, the Bible never teaches, explicitly or implicitly, the idea of prevenient grace.

2. If a person's will is not affected either by predisposition or outside influence, then it is completely arbitrary. Arbitrary choices are not truly free.

LIBERTARIAN FREE WILL

50%   50%

3. The Bible teaches that people's choices are affected by other people's choices.

Deuteronomy 20:5
"You shall not worship them or serve them; for I, the LORD your God, am a jealous God, visiting the iniquity of the fathers on the children, on the third and the fourth generations of those who hate Me."

Mark 9:42
"Whoever causes one of these little ones who believe to stumble, it would be better for him if, with a heavy millstone hung around his neck, he had been cast into the sea."

PELAGIAN FREE WILL

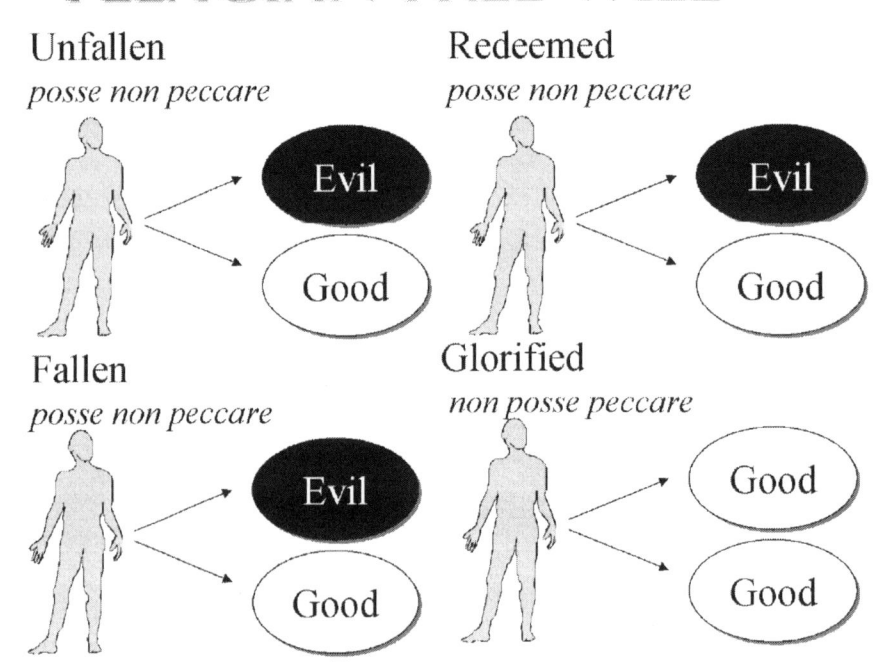

Unfallen
posse non peccare
→ Evil
→ Good

Redeemed
posse non peccare
→ Evil
→ Good

Fallen
posse non peccare
→ Evil
→ Good

Glorified
non posse peccare
→ Good
→ Good

ARMINIAN FREE WILL

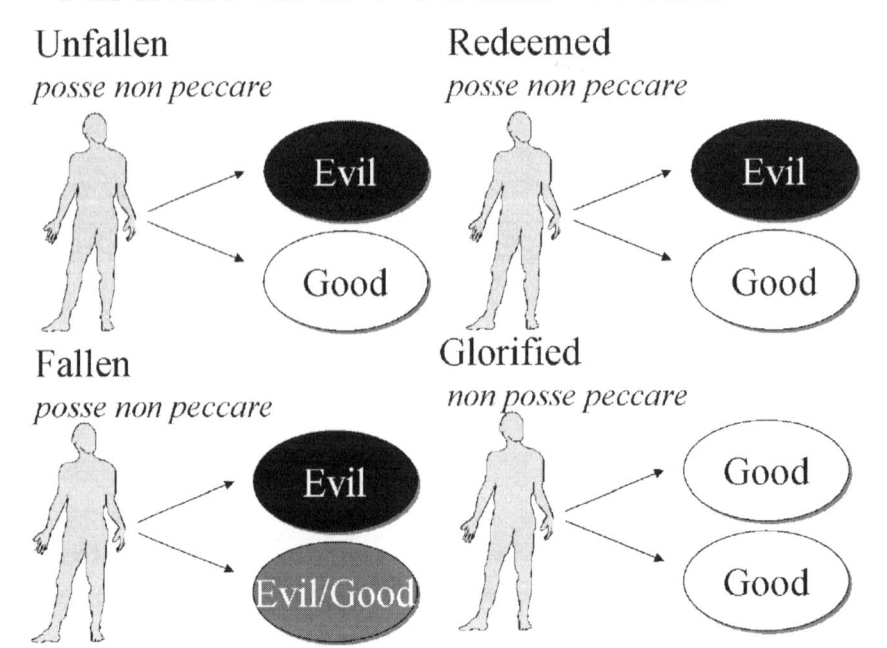

Unfallen
posse non peccare
→ Evil
→ Good

Redeemed
posse non peccare
→ Evil
→ Good

Fallen
posse non peccare
→ Evil
→ Evil/Good

Glorified
non posse peccare
→ Good
→ Good

SESSION 8: FREE WILL

AUGUSTINIAN FREE WILL

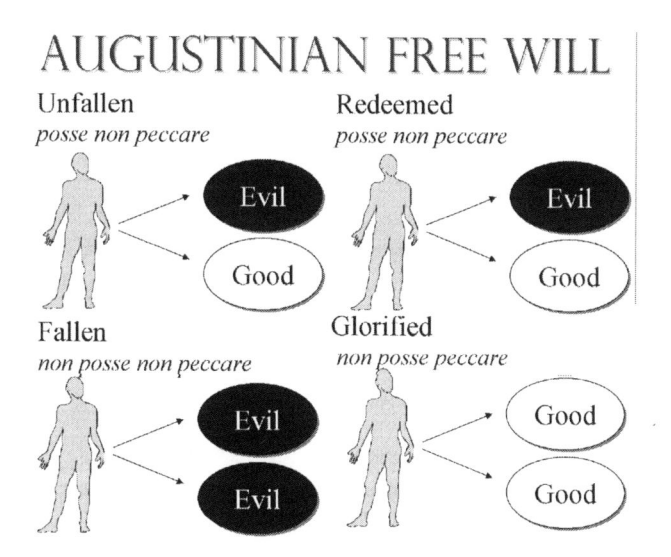

Unfallen — *posse non peccare* → Evil, Good

Redeemed — *posse non peccare* → Evil, Good

Fallen — *non posse non peccare* → Evil, Evil

Glorified — *non posse peccare* → Good, Good

Free Will: Is there such a thing?

Yes and no. No, if you mean that we have libertarian freedom, or freedom to choose against our nature (what Augustine defined as liberty). Yes, if you mean that we will always be free to choose according to our greatest desire. We are bound by the inclinations of our nature to such a degree that we would never choose against it.

Summary

• Man's will is free in the sense that he is free to do what he is able to do. In other words, man's free will is limited by his ability.

• Man has the natural ability to make choices but lacks the ability to make Godly choices.

• Man cannot make any move toward God on his own since his will is in bondage and at enmity against God in its natural state.

John 6:44
"No one can come to me unless the Father who sent me draws him."

John 8:34-36
"Jesus answered them, 'Truly, truly, I say to you, everyone who commits sin is the slave of sin. The slave does not remain in the house forever; the son does remain forever. So if the Son makes you free, you will be free indeed.'"

Romans 8:16-23
"Do you not know that when you present yourselves to someone as slaves for obedience, you are slaves of the one whom you obey, either of sin resulting in death, or of obedience resulting in righteousness? But thanks be to God that though you were slaves of sin, you became obedient from the heart to that form of teaching to which you were committed, and having been freed from sin, you became slaves of righteousness. I am speaking in human terms because of the weakness of your flesh. For just as you presented your members as slaves to impurity and to lawlessness, resulting in further lawlessness, so now present your members as slaves to righteousness, resulting in sanctification. For when you were slaves of sin, you were free in regard to righteousness. Therefore what benefit were you then deriving from the things of which you are now ashamed? For the outcome of those things is death. But now having been freed from sin and enslaved to God, you derive your benefit, resulting in sanctification, and the outcome, eternal life. For the wages of sin is death, but the free gift of God is eternal life in Christ Jesus our Lord."

Luke 6:45
"The good man out of the good treasure of his heart brings forth what is good; and the evil man out of the evil treasure brings forth what is evil; for his mouth speaks from that which fills his heart."

SESSION 8: FREE WILL

POSTSCRIPT: ORIGINAL SIN

How can we be held guilty for the sin of another?

Question: Is it fair and righteous to have the sin of another counted against us and have our nature corrupted to such a degree that all of our inclinations are toward evil? Isn't original sin unjust?

> "Without doubt, nothing is more shocking to our reason than to say that the sin of the first man has implicated in its guilt men so far from the original sin that they seem incapable of sharing it. This flow of guilt does not seem merely impossible to us, but indeed most unjust. What could be more contrary to the rules of our miserable justice than the eternal damnation of a child, incapable of will, for an act in which he seems to have so little part that it was actually committed 6,000 years before he existed? Certainly nothing jolts us more rudely than this doctrine . . ."
>
> —Blaise Pascal
>
> Pensees, Trans A.J. Krailsheimer (Harmondswrth: Penguin Books, 1966), 65.

St. Thomas Aquinas' theory on the redemption of Angels.

GROUP DISCUSSION QUESTIONS

1. The concept of free will is notoriously difficult to define. It is a concept that is often used in Christian circles, but seldom articulated and understood. Having been through this session, how would you define free will?

2. Do you believe that libertarian freedom is possible? How?

3. Discuss the outside factors in your life that were beyond your control. How have these factors made you what you are?

4. Can it be said that you have true freedom when these factors are considered? Please explain.

SESSION 8: FREE WILL

5. One of the objections to libertarianism is that if a person's will is not affected either by predisposition or outside influence, then it is completely arbitrary. Arbitrary choices are not truly free. Do you agree? Why or why not.

6. It is said by compatibilists that because of the fall and our outside influences, we do not have true liberty. However, we do make free choices and therefore are responsible for those choices. Do you agree? Why or why not.

7. If compatibilism were true, why would God still find fault in man if He is the first cause that placed him in the circumstances that have determined his choices?

8. How was your thinking most challenged by the lesson? Please explain.

Session 9

THE SEX OF HUMANITY: EGALITARIANISM

Men and Women: What's the difference?

Men and Women: What do you love and hate about yourself?

To the women: What do you like most about being a woman?
To the men: What do you like most about being a man?
To the women: What would you like least about being a woman?
To the men: What would you like least about being a man?

Read Genesis 2:18-25

Two Positions:

    1. Egalitarianism

    2. Complementarianism

> "A woman, however learned and holy, may not take upon herself to teach in an assembly of men."
> —the Synod of Carthage, A.D. 398

> "Many women have received power through the grace of God and performed many deeds of manly valor."
> —Clement of Alexandria

> "You are the Devil's gateway; you are the unsealer of that tree; you are the first forsaker of the divine law; you are the one who persuaded him whom the Devil was not brave enough to approach."
> —Tertullian

> "A woman must quietly receive instruction with entire submissiveness. But I do not allow a woman to teach or exercise authority over a man, but to remain quiet. For it was Adam who was first created, *and* then Eve. And *it was* not Adam *who* was deceived, but the woman being deceived, fell into transgression. But *women* will be preserved through the bearing of children if they continue in faith and love and sanctity with self-restraint."
> —Paul, 1 Tim. 2:11-15

SESSION 9: EGALITARIANISM

What is Egalitarianism?

Egalitarianism: The Bible does not teach that women are in any sense, functionally or ontologically, subservient to men. Women and men hold ministry positions according to their gifts, not their gender. The principle of mutual submission teaches that husbands and wives are to submit to each other equally.

Adherents: N.T. Wight, Gregory Boyd, Stanley Grenz, Richard Foster, Gorden Fee, Craig Keener

Defense of Egalitarianism:

1. Patriarchalism (male domination) is a cultural phenomenon that God chose not to deal with, but to regulate as he also did with slavery.

Colossians 3:18-22
"Wives, be subject to your husbands, as is fitting in the Lord. Husbands, love your wives and do not be embittered against them. Children, be obedient to your parents in all things, for this is well-pleasing to the Lord. Fathers, do not exasperate your children, so that they will not lose heart. Slaves, in all things obey those who are your masters on earth, not with external service, as those who merely please men, but with sincerity of heart, fearing the Lord."

2. Male leadership and domination is a result of the fall that is reversed when we are restored in Christ.

Genesis. 3:16
"To the woman He said, 'I will greatly multiply Your pain in childbirth, in pain you will bring forth children; yet your desire will be for your husband, and he will rule over you.'"

Galatians 3:28
"There is neither Jew nor Greek, there is neither slave nor free man, there is neither male nor female; for you are all one in Christ Jesus."

3. The Bible has many examples of women who were leaders, teachers, and prophetesses who exercised authority over men.

- Miriam is stated to be a leader of the Exodus alongside Moses and Aaron (Micah 6:4).
- Deborah served as a judge in Israel (Judges 4-5).
- Huldah was a prophetess consulted by both men and women (2 Kings 22:14).
- There were prophetesses in the New Testament who carried the authority of their office teaching men (Luke 2:36-38; Acts 2:16-18; 21:8-9; 1 Cor. 11:4-5).
- History has conclusively demonstrated that women have been very effective spiritual leaders and pastors.

  -Catharine Booth
  -Joan of Arc
  -Amy Carmichael
  -Corrie Ten Boon
  -Elisabeth Elliott
  -Joyce Meyers

4. Despite claims to the contrary, it is hard to see how stating that women are denied the opportunity of exercising spiritual headship over men does not demean the ontological value of women.

Response to Egalitarianism:

1. While it is true that God sometimes does not reform cultural issues immediately, a husband's leadership is not a cultural issue any morethan children obeying their parents (Eph. 6:1) is a cultural issue.

2. There is much evidence that clearly shows that male leadership is not a result of the Fall:

- Adam was created first.
- Eve was created as a completer.
- Adam named Eve.
- God spoke to Adam first after the Fall.
- Adam, not Eve, represents the human race in the Fall (Rom. 5:12-19).
- The curse brought distortion of previous roles, not the introduction of new role.

3. Many of the examples, such as Deborah, are the exception because of the lack of male leadership. Women, however, did effectively prophesy and hold leadership positions in the early church and can in today's church as well. The debate is not whether women can be leaders or teachers, but whether they can be in authority over men.

4. Again, it is agreed that women have been and are very effective leaders. But referring to the success of women who have occupied a position of spiritual leadership over men is pragmatic at best. God may bless ministries in spite of their shortcomings and not because of them.

5. Stating that people are genetically prepared for particular services is not a dishonor and it does not promote an ontological hierarchy. Acknowledgement is easily made that men are not prepared for childbirth, but this in no way devalues their person; it just substantiates that their role is not childbearing.

GROUP DISCUSSION QUESTIONS

1. To the women: What do you like most about being a woman?

2. To the men: What do you like most about being a man?

3. To the women: What would you like least about being a woman?

4. To the men: What would you like least about being a man?

5. What arguments of the egalitarian position do you find most compelling?

SESSION 9: EGALITARIANISM

6. This was one of the egalitarian arguments. "Despite claims to the contrary, it is hard to see how stating that women are denied the opportunity of exercising spiritual headship over men does not demean the ontological value of women." Do you agree with this statement? Why or why not?

7. Do you believe that women can be pastors over a congregation? Why or why not?

8. Do you believe that there is any situation in which women can teach men? Please explain.

9. How was your thinking most challenged by the lesson? Please explain.

Session 10

THE SEX OF HUMANITY: COMPLEMENTARIANISM
Created equal and different

What is Complementarianism?

Complementarianism: The Bible teaches that men and women are of equal worth, dignity, and responsibility before God (ontological equality). The Bible also teaches that men and women have different roles to play in society, the family, and the church. These roles do not compete but complement each other.

Adherents: Wayne Grudem, John Piper, Douglas Moo, Charles Swindoll, John MacArthur

Defense of Complementarianism:

1. The Bible illustrates male leadership from the beginning of creation.

- Adam named the animals (Genesis 2:20).
- Adam named Eve (Genesis 2:23).
- God approached Adam first after the fall (Genesis 2:9).
- There were no women priests.
- The God-ordained rulers of Israel were male.
- Jesus' apostles were all male.
- The bishops/presbyters/pastors were all male
(1 Timothy 3:2; Titus1:6).

2. Eve was created as a completer. In order for one to be incomplete, he or she must lack something. Adam lacked something that caused God to say, "It is not good for man to be alone" (Genesis 2:18). Eve was created to complete that which was lacking. It is important to realize that she was not simply a second attempt at perfection. Eve was created with essential characteristics that Adam did not have. Likewise, Adam was created with characteristics that Eve did not have. They were created to complement each other. Therefore, the role distinction is essential for humanity to be complete.

3. Paul constantly had to address women who were failing to understand the importance of their role as women or who were in outright rebellion against it. These women were blurring the God-ordained roles and attempting to usurp the role of man. This rebellion is part of the curse.

> **Genesis 3:16**
> "To the woman He said, 'I will greatly multiply your pain in childbirth, in pain you will bring forth children; yet you will want to control you husband, and he will rule over you.'"
>
> **1 Timothy 2:12-15**
> "But I do not allow a woman to teach or exercise authority over a man, but to remain quiet. For it was Adam who was first created, and then Eve. And it was not Adam who was deceived, but the woman being deceived, fell into transgression. But women will be preserved through the bearing of children if they continue in faith and love and sanctity with self-restraint."
>
> **1 Corinthians 14:34-35**
> "The women are to keep silent in the churches; for they are not permitted to speak, but are to subject themselves, just as the Law also says. If they desire to learn anything, let them ask their own husbands at home; for it is improper for a woman to speak in church."
>
> **1 Corinthians 11:3**
> "But I want you to understand that Christ is the head of every man, and the man is the head of a woman, and God is the head of Christ."

SESSION 10: COMPLEMENTARIANISM

> Colossians 3:18
> "Wives, submit to your husbands, as is fitting in the Lord."
>
> **Titus 2:5**
> "[Women are] to be sensible, pure, workers at home, kind, being subject to their own husbands, so that the word of God will not be dishonored."

4. The New Testament writers constantly had to address men who abused their role as leaders. This is part of the curse. The instruction to men, however, is not to stop leading, but to lead in a way that is sensitive, encouraging, and loving.

> **Genesis 3:16**
> "To the woman He said, 'I will greatly multiply your pain in childbirth, in pain you will bring forth children; yet your desire will be for your husband, and he will rule over you.'"
>
> **Ephesians 5:25a, 28, 33a**
> "Husbands, love your wives, just as Christ also loved the church and gave Himself up for her. . . . So husbands ought also to love their own wives as their own bodies. He who loves his own wife loves himself. . . . Nevertheless, each individual among you also is to love his own wife even as himself . . ."
>
> **1 Peter 3:7**
> "You husbands in the same way, live with your wives in an understanding way, as with someone weaker, since she is a woman; and show her honor as a fellow heir of the grace of life, so that your prayers will not be hindered."
>
> **Colossians 3:19**
> "Husbands, love your wives and do not be harsh with them."

5. Most of church history has adhered to a complementarian view.

Response to Complementarianism:

1. These illustrations of male leadership were descriptive, not prescriptive. In other words, male leadership, like slavery, was a cultural phenomenon that God chose not to overthrow at the time.

2. While it is agreed that the woman was created to complete humanity (not man), this does not necessitate that God intended a functional hierarchy. Male leadership, rulership, domination, whatever name it goes by, was a product of the Fall, not creation.

3. Paul was writing to cultural situations that do not demand universal application. For example, when Paul wrote to Timothy in Ephesus, there were women who were formerly cult prostitutes and uneducated (typically only receiving secondhand instruction from their husbands) who were attempting to "fill the pulpit." He uses Eve to illustrate how destructive secondhand information can be. He does not use the events in the Garden as a universal principle. Paul's command here, is then purely cultural.

4. These passages in the New Testament do not regulate how husbands are to rule, but do instruct on how they are to relate. They are to love their wives and not rule over them.

5. It is a sad fact that the history of the Church is littered with abusive relationships coming from man's sinful tendency to dominate. Christians abused the Jews, they justified slavery, and they forced people to convert during the Inquisitions. Any appeal to history carries little weight in these areas and might even work against the complementarian view.

SESSION 10: COMPLEMENTARIANISM

> *"Of two-hundred and fifty cultures studies, males dominate in almost all. Males are almost always the rule makers, hunters, builders, fashioners of weapons, workers in metal, wood, or stone. Women are mostly care givers and most involved in child rearing. . . . The fact that these universals transcend divergent animal groups and cultures suggests that there must be predeterminants of gender-related behavior."*
>
> —Gregg Johnson
>
> Wayne Grudem and John Piper ed. *Recovering Biblical Manhood and Womanhood* (Wheaton, IL: Crossway, 1991), 281

Biological Differences Between the Sexes

Women:

- Store more fat and retain more heat.
- Have more white blood cells and B and T lymphocytes (can fight off infection faster).
- Are more perceptive due to a more responsive sensory system: finer body hair, more acute sense of hearing, taste, touch, and smell.
- Can discriminate color better (particularly on the red end of the spectrum).
- Have less testosterone (are more patient, stay in immediate family longer).
- A baby's cry triggers involuntary responses.
- Produce more cortisol during prolonged stressful situations. (Cortisol reduces the serotonin which can lead to depression.)

Men:

- Have ten percent higher metabolic rate.
- Have fifty percent more muscle mass.
- Have more sweat glands to dissipate heat faster.
- Have ten percent more red blood cells (wounds heal faster).
- Have fifteen times higher testosterone after puberty (more aggressive, sexually active, enjoy competitive sports, leave immediate family earlier, and are prone to argue).
- Produce more testosterone during prolonged stressful times giving more endurance, but are more apt to have hypertension.

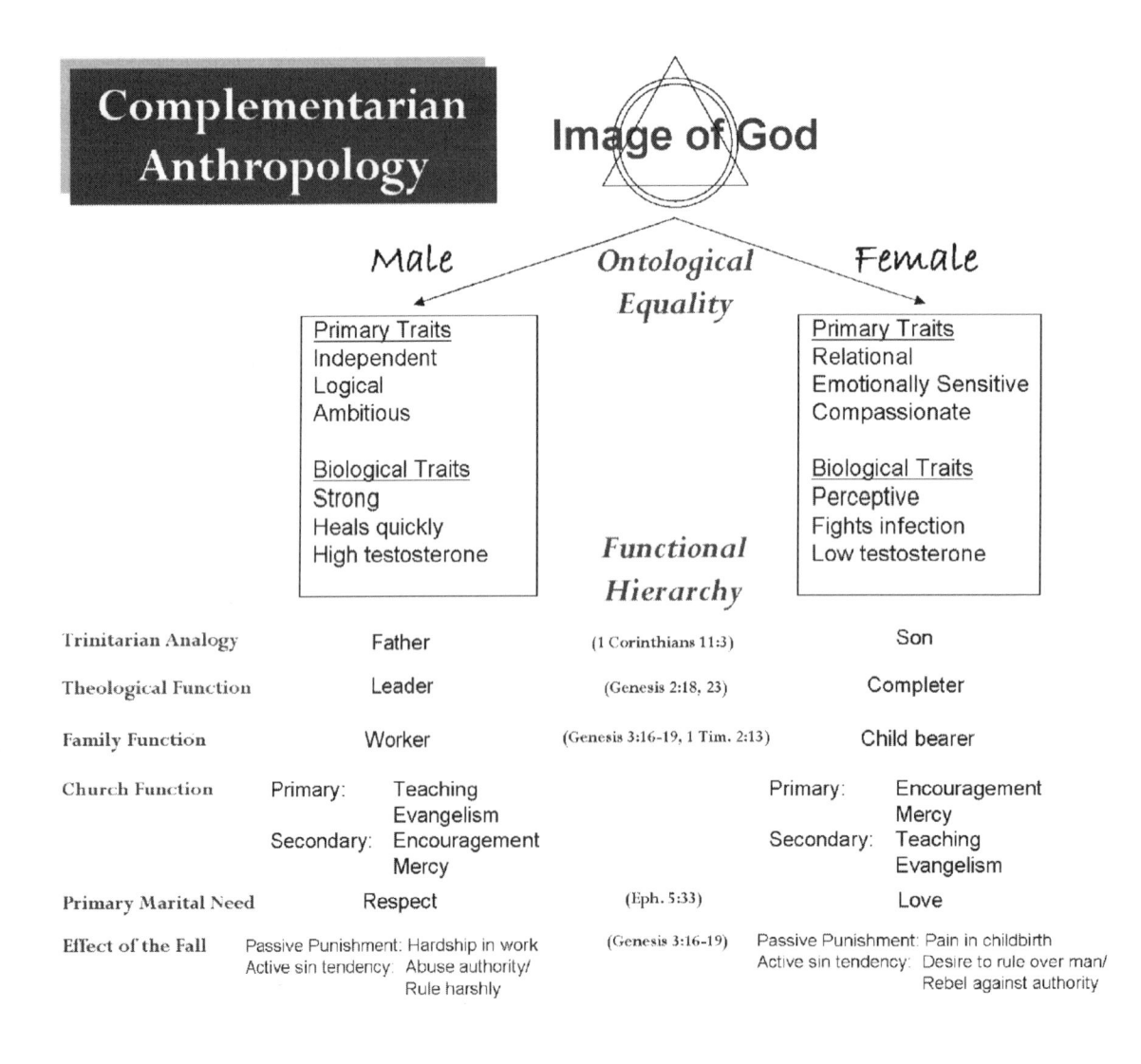

Complementarian Anthropology

Image of God

Male — *Ontological Equality* — *Female*

Male
Primary Traits
- Independent
- Logical
- Ambitious

Biological Traits
- Strong
- Heals quickly
- High testosterone

Female
Primary Traits
- Relational
- Emotionally Sensitive
- Compassionate

Biological Traits
- Perceptive
- Fights infection
- Low testosterone

Functional Hierarchy

	Male		Female
Trinitarian Analogy	Father	(1 Corinthians 11:3)	Son
Theological Function	Leader	(Genesis 2:18, 23)	Completer
Family Function	Worker	(Genesis 3:16-19, 1 Tim. 2:13)	Child bearer
Church Function	Primary: Teaching, Evangelism / Secondary: Encouragement, Mercy		Primary: Encouragement, Mercy / Secondary: Teaching, Evangelism
Primary Marital Need	Respect	(Eph. 5:33)	Love
Effect of the Fall	Passive Punishment: Hardship in work / Active sin tendency: Abuse authority/ Rule harshly	(Genesis 3:16-19)	Passive Punishment: Pain in childbirth / Active sin tendency: Desire to rule over man/ Rebel against authority

SESSION 10: COMPLEMENTARIANISM

> "God has given each sex special gifts to carry out its task. This is not to argue that these gifts should only find expression in child rearing in the case of women or providing and protecting in the case of men. Yet it is out of this God-given design that these gifts arose and flourished. While today's technology may have reduced the need for such rigid division of labor, the gender gifts and aptitudes remain. . . . Our culture has changed, and the demands for traditional roles may have varied, yet our basic, God-given physiological differences have not. We excel at different gifts, and all the gifts are needed. Let us hope that, by recognizing the existence of gender differences, we can better understand each other and help to maximize each other's potentials. Likewise, by accepting our God-given gifts, we can resist cultural pressures to become what we are not and seek to master gifts we don't possess."
>
> —Gregg Johnson

Wayne Grudem and John Piper ed. *Recovering Biblical Manhood and Womanhood* (Wheaton, IL: Crossway, 1991), 293

> "People all around us are confused about who they are. Often in our attempt to honor God, we fail to realize the unique role God has given us in his kingdom. In this confusion, we vacillate between self-degradation and self-importance. Scripture, however, provides a balanced portrait of human beings. We are images of clay, but designed to represent the authority of the King of the universe. In this balanced perspective, we live with humility and dignity as images of God.
>
> —Richard Pratt

Richard Pratt, *Designed for Dignity* (Phillipsburg, NJ: P&R Publishing, 1993), 21

GROUP DISCUSSION QUESTIONS

1. What do you believe is the most compelling argument for the complementarian position?

2. Review this argument for complementarianism: "Eve was created as a completer. In order for one to be incomplete, he or she must lack something. Adam lacked something that caused God to say, "It is not good for man to be alone" (Genesis 2:18). Eve was created to complete that which was lacking. It is important to realize that she was not simply a second attempt at perfection. Eve was created with essential characteristics that Adam did not have. Likewise, Adam was created with characteristics that Eve did not have. They were created to complement each other. Therefore, the role distinction is essential for humanity to be complete." What are your thoughts?

3. Having now heard the arguments for both positions, which do you find most compelling?

SESSION 10: COMPLEMENTARIANISM

4. Complementarians believe that their position is evidenced more prominently in Scripture and gives greater honor to women by recognizing their significance. Do you agree? Why or why not?

5. If men were to value the role of women as nurturers more, do you think that there would be a women's liberation movement like we see today? Please explain.

6. Men: How can you start honoring women more?

7. Women: How can you find more dignity in your role?

8. How was your thinking most challenged by the lesson? Please explain.

The Early Church Fathers 90–500

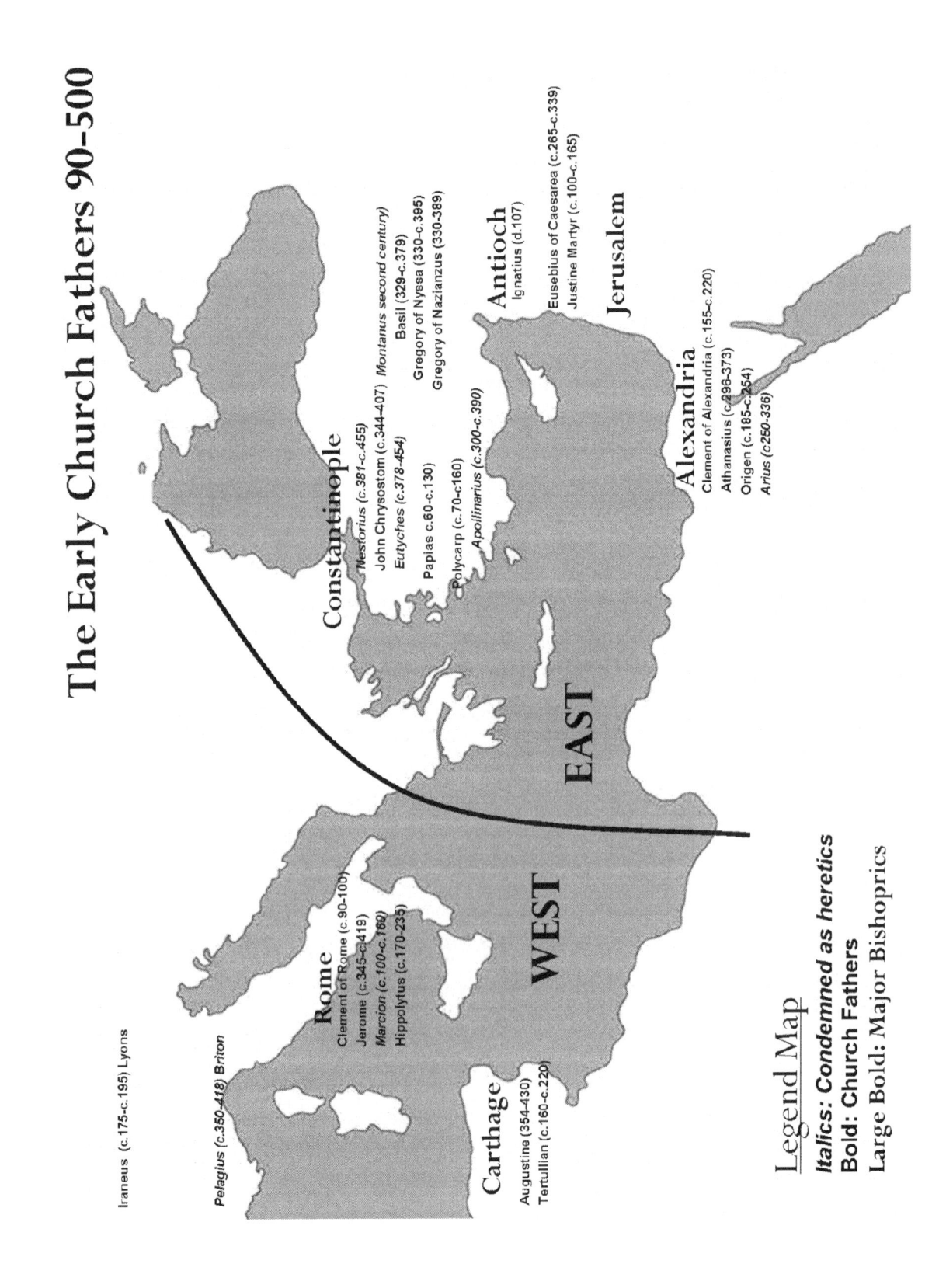

Constantinople
Nestorius (c.381-c.455)
John Chrysostom (c.344-407) *Montanus second century*
Eutyches (c.378-454) Basil (329-c.379)
Papias c.60-c.130 Gregory of Nyssa (330-c.395)
Polycarp (c.70-c160) Gregory of Nazianzus (330-389)
Apollinarius (c.300-c.390)

Antioch
Ignatius (d.107)
Eusebius of Caesarea (c.265-c.339)
Justine Martyr (c.100-c.165)

Jerusalem

Alexandria
Clement of Alexandria (c.155-c.220)
Athanasius (c.296-373)
Origen (c.185-c.254)
Arius (c250-336)

Iraneus (c.175-c.195) Lyons

Pelagius (c.350-418) Briton

Rome
Clement of Rome (c. 90-100)
Jerome (c.345-c.419)
Marcion (c.100-c.160)
Hippolytus (c.170-235)

WEST

EAST

Carthage
Augustine (354-430)
Tertullian (c.160-c.220)

Legend Map
Italics: Condemned as heretics
Bold: Church Fathers
Large Bold: Major Bishoprics

APPENDIX 1:
THE DOCTRINE OF ORIGINAL SIN
Are we really condemned for another man's sin?

The concept of "Original Sin" has long been a vital part of Christian Orthodoxy. Perhaps John Calvin defines Original Sin most concisely as "The depravation of a nature formerly good and pure."[1] More specifically, it refers to the fall of humanity from its original state of innocence and purity to a state of guilt, depravation, and corruption. It is the cause of man's translation from a state of unbroken communion before God to one of spiritual death. The how and when of this transmission of corruption is more difficult to define. In fact, the term "Original Sin" is not found in Scripture; Saint Augustine coined it in the 4th century.[2] The primary passage used to defend the doctrine of Original Sin is Romans 5:12-21.

> 12"Therefore, just as through one man sin entered into the world, and death through sin, and so death spread to all men, because all sinned—13for until the Law sin was in the world, but sin is not imputed when there is no law. 14Nevertheless death reigned from Adam until Moses, even over those who had not sinned in the likeness of the offense of Adam, who is a type of Him who was to come. 15But the free gift is not l like the transgression. For if by the transgression of the one the many died, much more did the grace of God and the gift by the grace of the one Man, Jesus Christ, abound to the many. 16The gift is not like that which came through the one who sinned; for on the one hand the judgment arose from one transgression resulting in condemnation, but on the other hand the free gift arose from many transgressions resulting in justification. 17For if by the transgression of the one, death reigned through the one, much more those who receive the abundance of grace and of the gift of righteousness will reign in life through the One, Jesus Christ. 18So then as through one transgression there resulted condemnation to all men, even so through one act of righteousness there resulted justification of life to all men. 19For as through the one man's disobedience the many were made sinners, even so through the obedience of the One the many will be made righteous. 20The Law came in so that the transgression would increase; but where sin increased, grace abounded all the more, 21so

---
[1] John Calvin, Institutes, book 2, 1:5 (Logos Electronic Database).
[2] Packer, J. I., Concise Theology, (Wheaton, Illinois: Tyndale House, 1993) Logos.

that, as sin reigned in death, even so grace would reign through righteousness to eternal life through Jesus Christ our Lord" (NAS).

Most specifically, Romans 5:12 gives us the most explicit reference to this concept: "Therefore, just as through one man sin entered into the world, and death through sin, and so death spread to all men, because all sinned." The "one man" is Adam. The "all men" is all of Adam's posterity—the entire human race.

J.I. Packer clears up a possible misconception and further defines Original Sin:[1]

> The assertion of original sin means not that sin belongs to human nature as God made it (God made mankind upright, Ecclesiastes 7:29), nor that sin is involved in the processes of reproduction and birth (the uncleanness connected with menstruation, semen, and childbirth in Leviticus 12 and 15 was typical and ceremonial only, not moral and real), but that . . . sinfulness marks everyone from birth . . . it derives to us in a real . . . mysterious way from Adam, our first representative before God.[3]

This concept is not only hard to understand, but it is also quite disturbing. To state that we are condemned for the sin of another is not only offensive and unfair, but in the mind of most it is also ludicrous. It is because of this that Pascal wrote the following:

> Without doubt, nothing is more shocking to our reason than to say that the sin of the first man has[2] implicated in its guilt men so far from the original sin that they seem incapable of sharing it. This flow of guilt does not seem merely impossible to us, but indeed most unjust. What could be more contrary to the rules of our miserable justice than the eternal damnation of a child, incapable of will, for an act in which he seems to have so little part that it was actually committed 6,000 years before he existed? Certainly nothing jolts us more rudely than this doctrine . . .[4]

It certainly does seem unfair for us to be blamed for the sin of another. My little niece used to commit various misdemeanors such as messing up the living

---

3 Ibid.
4 Blaise Pascal, Pensees, Trans A.J. Krailsheimer (Harmondswrth: Penguin Books, 1966), 65.

room. She would find solace in her younger brother, who was not yet able to speak and defend himself. She would blame him for the mess that she had made, which, of course, was not right. Unfortunately, she got away with it many times before her parents caught on. Her brother was therefore punished for crimes he did not commit. Is it the same with Adam and humanity? Are we being punished for a sin that we had nothing to do with?

Death, Paul says, is passed down to us from Adam. But there is more to it than that. As Pyne puts it, "We have no problem affirming that all people die, but what did Paul mean when he linked death to sin?"[5] Furthermore, physical death is not the only consequence of Adam's sin that we inherit. Romans 5:18 states that the transgression of Adam resulted in our condemnation. So then, we are not only destined to die because of Adam's sin, but we are also condemned to eternal death.[6]

Was the sin of Adam transferred to us? If so, how? Are we condemned for the sin of another? Are Pascal's concerns valid? If not, why does Paul say in Romans that, "Through one transgression there resulted condemnation to all men" (Romans 5:18)? Let's boil these down to the following two key[1] related questions: Did you or I have anything to do with Adam's sin being so far removed from it? What does Paul mean when he said "all sinned"?[7]

Here we will attempt to answer these questions. First, we will look at how the Church through the centuries has dealt with this problem. Second, we will take a closer look at the passage in ques[2]tion and attempt to narrow our interpretive options. Finally, we will make a synthesis by taking into account the possible interpretations along with the theological implications of each.

---

5 Robert Pyne, Humanity and Sin, (Nashville, TN: Word, 1999), 164.
6 That condemnation and death are not the same is evident from Paul's usage in this passage.
7 John Murray, WTJ, vol. 18, 150

History of Original Sin[1]

Pelagianism

The doctrine of Original Sin was not adequately dealt with among the early Church Fathers. The first time substantial discussion arose was at the time of Augustine (354-430). Augustine held that man is unable to do any good because man is inherently depraved. Augustine believed that all men are born with a predisposition to sin. This is what led him to his strong promotion of the necessity of predestination. "Give what thou command," said Augustine, "and command what thou wilt." At this time, believing Augustine's position to be unfair and extreme, a British monk named Pelagius (c. 354- after 418) denied that Original Sin was passed on from Adam to the human race. As to his interpretation of Romans 5:12, Pelagius believed that, "As Adam sinned and therefore died so in a like manner all men die because they sin."[2] According to Pelagius, we inherit Adam's sin neither by imputation of guilt nor by nature. The only effect that Adam had on the human race is the example he set. In the view of Pelagius, all men are born neutral in a like manner to Adam with no predisposition to evil. Pelagius was eventually condemned by two African councils in 416 and by the council of Ephesus in 431. In spite of his condemnation, the Pelagian doctrine of sin is still prominent in the Church today.

Arminians

Jacob Arminius believed that all men are considered guilty only when they partake in sin by their own free will in the same manner as Adam did. As Enns put it, "When people would voluntarily and purposefully choose to sin even though they had power to live righteously—then, and only then, would God impute sin to them

---

1 Although many theories will be examined here, their separation does not imply complete and total distinction. It is understood that many of the following proposed explanations of Romans 5:12 are agglomerated and combined by many theologians to form various theories.
2 Murray, 151

and count them guilty."[1] Therefore, the sinful state is transmitted by natural generation, while the condemnation for the actual sin is only transmitted by partaking of sin in a like manner.

Augustinianism

Many theologians[2] have proposed a theory called Augustinianism (also called "realism," or "seminalism"). This theory has traditionally been linked with Augustine and has most recently been staunchly defended by Shedd. According to an Augustinian interpretation of Romans 5:12, "all sinned" in that all humanity was physically present in Adam when he sinned.[3] "[Those who hold to the Augustinian view of Original Sin] insist that we can be held accountable only for what we have actually done.[4] As Shedd puts it, "The first sin of Adam, being a common, not an individual sin, is deservedly and justly imputed to the posterity of Adam upon the same principle which all sin is deservingly and justly imputed: namely, that it was committed by those to whom it is imputed." [5]This view is attractive in that it takes literally Paul's statement that "all sinned."

Federalism

The federal view of humanity's relationship to Adam proposes that Adam was selected by God to be humanity's federal representative. This view was first proposed by Cocceius (1603-1669) and is the standard belief of Reformed theology. As Achan's family was held responsible for his sin (Joshua 7:16-26), so it[6]

---

1 Enns, Paul, The Moody Handbook of Theology, (Chicago, Ill.: Moody Press, 1996), 312.
2 L. Chafer, Shedd, Calvin, Luther, Augustine.
3 Support for this theory given from Heb 7:9-10 where Levi is said to pay tithes to Melchizedek although Levi was still not born: "And, so to speak, through Abraham even Levi, who received tithes, paid tithes, for he was still in the loins of his father when Melchizedek met him."
4 Pyne, 166.

5 Shedd, Dogmatic Theology Vol. 2 (Minneapolis, MN: Klock and Klock, 1979), 186.
6 Enns, 312.

is with Adam's family. By this view, the "all sinned" of Romans 5:12 would not be taken literally. As Ryrie puts it, "No one but Adam actually committed that first sin, but since Adam represented all people, God viewed all as involved and thus condemned."[1] The reason that Adam's sin is imputed to his posterity according to the federalist is because God imputes the guilt of Adam, whom He chose to represent mankind, to mankind.

Interpretation of Romans 5:12-21

The way in which one interprets this passage will determine which of the above options he or she adopts. The context of the passage has Paul explaining the believer's position in Christ by comparing it to our former position in Adam. The subject of the section is not the transgression, but the free gift (v. 15). Paul uses the analogy of Adam's sin and compares it to the free gift of Christ's righteousness.

The meaning of the phrase, "because all sinned"[2] (NAS) is the primary subject of debate. Read it once more. What is the meaning of "all sinned"? It cannot be that all people sin as an act of their own choice (contra Pelagius) or because of their inherited nature (contra the Arminian interpretation). Why? It is because of the force of the verb tense. If the Pelagian or Arminian interpretation were correct, the present tense would have been a much better choice for Paul. Then it would naturally read, "Because all sin." Then we could answer the question "Why are all people condemned?" with "Because all people sin." But this is not the case here in Romans. It clearly states that "all sinned" (past tense; Greek historic aorist tense). Therefore, we are connected with the past sin of Adam. As Morris has it, "The aorist

---

[1] Ryrie, Basic Theology (Wheaton, IL: Victor, 1982), 224.
[2] That evfV w - should be interpreted with the causal is seen in its idiomatic usage elsewhere in the NT: 2 Corinthians 5:4 "For indeed while we are in this tent, we groan, being burdened, because (evfV w) we do not want to be unclothed but to be clothed . . ." See also Douglas Moo, NICNT The Epistle to the Romans (Grand Rapids, MI: Eerdmans, 1996), 322; and Wallace, GGBB (Grand Rapids, MI: Zondervan, 1996), 342-343.

[tense] points to one act, the act of Adam; we would expect the present or the imperfect [tense] if the Apostle were thinking of the continuing sins of all people."[1]

Verse 12 begins the comparison of Adam with Christ. Paul then feels inclined to break off on one of his all-too-common parenthetical statements in verses 13-14 to defend his statement "because all sinned." This is important because Paul's understanding of what "all sinned" means is wrapped up in his defense which follows. Verse 13 begins with the conjunction "for" (gar). This links it with the previous statement, "because all sinned." It is as if someone got the impression that Paul was stating that all people sin, and therefore all people die as a consequence of their own sin. At this point (v. 13), Paul says that before the Law, there was sin. But people did not die on account of these personal sins, because they were not imputed as sin ("but sin is not imputed when there is no law" v. 13). Then the objection may be "How do you explain that all people still died before the law?" Paul is stating that the reason people died before they commit an act of sin is because they are suffering the consequences of a sin already committed. They died not for personal sin, but for imputed sin. This sin was the sin of Adam. All people die because of the one sin of Adam.

Paul returns to his comparison to expound further. This comparison is between two things:

1. The effects of Adam's sin

2. The effects of Christ's righteousness

Whatever one does with Christ's righteousness, one must do to Adam's sin. [2] First let us draw out the comparison so that it might be better seen.

---

[1] Leon Morris, The Epistle to the Romans (Grand Rapid, MI: Eerdmans, 1987), 231-232.
[2] This of course must be limited to means or manner, not to the number of participants involved. Adam's sin was given to all mankind, while Christ's righteousness is limited to those who believe in Christ.

Through Adam's Sin	Through Christ's Righteousness
Judgment (16)	Free gift (16)
Condemnation (16)	Justification (16)
Death Reigned (17)	Life Reigned (17)
One Transgression=Condemnation of all (18)	One Act of Righteousness=Justification of all (18)
Adam's disobedience=many were made sinners (19)	Christ's obedience=many were made righteous (19)

The comparison is unmistakable. Whatever we do to inherit the free gift is the same thing we did to inherit judgment (v. 16). This is the force of the "just as" (hosper) in v. 12. Whatever we do to receive justification is the same thing we did to receive condemnation (v. 16). The effects of the "one act of righteousness" are brought about by the same means as the "condemnation of all men" (v. 18). The way in which believers are made righteous is analogous to the way all mankind was made sinners (v. 19). In order to answer the question as to how it is that "all sinned" and all were condemned in Adam, we must answer the question as to how Christ's righteousness is applied to us to the end that we are justified by that righteousness.[1]

If we were to adopt the view as held by Pelagius, that Adam's sin has no effect upon us whatsoever and that only his example has given us trouble, this means that Christ's righteousness has no effect upon us either. He simply came to set the example. But this is not what the text teaches. It states that the many were made sinners and that the many were made righteous. The effect of these two men's acts goes far beyond that of an example.

If we were to state, as the Arminians do, that we have Adam's sin imputed to us only when we act in the same manner as Adam did, then we must state that we

---

[1] See Murray, vol. 19, 36

have Christ's righteousness imputed to us only when we act as Christ acted. This cannot be true seeing as how we inherit Christ's righteousness while we are sinners (Rom 5:8, 10).

If one were to opt for a purely Augustinian interpretation of the passage in that we all actually and realistically sinned in Adam, then we would also have to concede that we all actually and realistically were righteous in Christ. This, of course, will not do for the analogy would be rendered meaningless and would contradict Paul's doctrine of justification by faith alone (Rom 3:28; Eph 2:8-9).

Paul is attempting to explain our relationship to Christ's righteousness by comparing it to the imputation of Adam's sin to us. This relationship is best seen in the federal headship view of imputation. As Moo puts it, "Throughout this whole passage what Adam did and what Christ did are steadily held over against each other. Now salvation in Christ does not mean that we merit salvation by living good lives; rather, what Christ has done is significant. Just so, death in Adam does not mean that we are being punished for our own evil deeds; it is what Adam has done that is significant."[1]

Adam, as our chosen federal head, has represented us and passed on sin and all of its consequences. Christ, as the second Adam, represents those who believe and passes on righteousness along with all its benefits. Christ's righteousness is given to us without any participation of our own, just as Adam's sin is given to us without our consent.

Synthesis

At this point it is important to ask the same questions that troubled us at beginning. As Pascal put it, the flow of guilt seems unjust. Seeing as how the most difficult interpretation of this section has been adopted and defended, how does one dodge the stumbling block that this interpretation proposes? How do we avoid the

---

[1] Douglas Moo, NITCNT The Epistle to the Romans (Grand Rapids, MI: Eerdmans, 1996), 232.

unfair conclusion that we are held guilty for the sin of another? Or do we just bite our tongue, hold our nose, and swallow it? Certainly, no one would complain about the fairness of the imputation of Christ righteousness, but the idea that condemnation is first imputed to all people with no distinction is difficult to grasp.

I would like to propose a possible explanation using St. Thomas Aquinas' hierarchy of angels. Aquinas developed a system of angels in which every angel is created of a distinct nature. According to Aquinas, there is no distinct species named "angels." What we refer to collectively as angels are actually all individually distinct creations of God with no spiritual or physical relation to one another. This is why Aquinas believed that there is no redemption for angels (Heb 2:16). If Christ were to redeem the angels, he would have to identify with the angels in all ways. Seeing as how each angel is a distinct species, he could not become one single species called "angels" in order to redeem the entire group, but he would have to become each individual angel and die for them one at a time.

Whether or not Aquinas' proposal about angels has any truth to it makes little difference for our present discussion. What is important is that Christ could become the species "man." Since man's being is linked with that of Adam in both physicality and spirituality, Christ could represent mankind all at once. Because we are vitally linked to the first Adam, we can be vitally linked to the second Adam, Jesus Christ.

At this point some may say that it is unfair because the proportions are different in those related to Adam and those related to Christ. While all men are related to the condemnation of Adam, not all men are related to the justification in Christ.

While this may be true, it might still be understood as a gracious act of God that we were all linked together with the first Adam. I propose that it was not a necessary act of God to link us with the first Adam. Nor do I believe that it was the natural outcome for Adam's posterity to be linked with him in death, sin, or condemnation. God, in theory, could have let each individual person have the same chance in the Garden, as he did with Adam. He could have caused each person to be born without any connection to Adam. Each would have been an individual creation who, if and when they sinned, would not be connected to anyone before or after. In this manner, the fall would come on an individual basis. Each person would be linked to only one person—himself or herself. Each person's condemnation would be his or her own. There would be no linkage to the rest of humanity. Each person would be spiritually and physically autonomous. This being the case, Christ could not represent "mankind," because there would be no solidarity to make this representation functional. We would be like the angels of Aquinas' hierarchy—without a Redeemer.

God, in his grace, knowing that when given the chance, each individual would follow Adam in his sin, declared all people guilty of Adam's, sin thereby creating a solidarity which was redeemable by a representative. Christ could only redeem mankind all at once, because mankind fell in Adam all at once. Therefore, God caused all men to sin in and with [1] Adam by an act of grace, knowing that all would choose the same as Adam. The "all sinned" in Romans 5:12 is as if Adam was in the Garden and held up the piece of fruit to a crowd which consisted of all mankind and shouted, "Should I eat it?" and the entire crowed shouted back, "Go for it!" In this, "all sinned."[2] God, then, in his grace, declared all guilty. The link was graciously made initially in Adam so that it might be made the second time in Christ.

---
[1] Terminology adopted from Moo, 326.
[2] It is understood that much of what has been proposed is speculative. It rests on the assumption that all men would have made the same choice as Adam, and that Christ would not have redeemed man any other way than through a representative fashion. Therefore, a disclaimer is made for the synthesis section of the paper, but no apology is necessary for the prior exegesis which created the stumbling block.

	Pelagius	**Arminian**	**Augustinianism** (Seminal/Realistic)	**Federalism** (Traditional Protestantism)
Meaning of "all sinned"	All sin in the same manner as Adam and therefore die.	All sin when they agree with Adam and sin thereby inheriting his guilt.	When Adam sinned, we sinned in him.	When Adam sinned, we sinned in and with him.
Mediate/ Immediate	Neither, no transferal of sin	Nature=Immediate Guilt=Mediate	Immediate	Immediate
Strengths	All people are responsible for only their own actions	We only inherit guilt by agreement	Recognizes the force of the passage. Heb 7:9-10 supports the idea.	Recognizes the force of the passage. Context and analogy supports this view.
Weaknesses	Does not recognize the force of the historic aorist nor the passage's emphasis on the one sin of Adam	Does not recognize the force of the historic aorist. Undue separation of guilt and nature.	The analogy of Christ and Adam does not support this view. If we actually sinned in Adam, we must have actually been righteous in Christ.	Difficult to see the justice in being punished for a sin that was not personally committed.

Appendix 2:

The Council of Orange
(529 AD)

Introduction:

The Council of Orange was an outgrowth of the controversy between Augustine and Pelagius. This controversy had to do with degree to which a human being is responsible for his or her own salvation, and the role of the grace of God in bringing about salvation. The Pelagians held that human beings are born in a state of innocence, i.e., that there is no such thing as a sinful nature or original sin.

As a result of this view, they held that a state of sinless perfection was achievable in this life. The Council of Orange dealt with the Semi-Pelagian doctrine that the human race, though fallen and possessed of a sinful nature, is still "good" enough to able to lay hold of the grace of God through an act of unredeemed human will. The Council held to Augustine's view and repudiated Pelagius. The following canons greatly influenced the Reformed doctrine of Total Depravity.[1]

CANON 1. If anyone denies that it is the whole man, that is, both body and soul, that was "changed for the worse" through the offense of Adam's sin, but believes that the freedom of the soul remains unimpaired and that only the body is subject to corruption, he is deceived by the error of Pelagius and contradicts the scripture which says, "The soul that sins shall die" (Ezek. 18:20); and, "Do you not know that if you yield yourselves to anyone as obedient slaves, you are the slaves of the one whom you obey?" (Rom. 6:16); and, "For whatever overcomes a man, to that he is enslaved" (2 Pet. 2:19).

CANON 2. If anyone asserts that Adam's sin affected him alone and not his descendants also, or at least if he declares that it is only the death of the body which is the punishment for sin, and not also that sin, which is the death of the soul, passed through one man to the whole human race, he does injustice to God and contradicts the Apostle, who says, "Therefore as sin came into the world through one man and death through sin, and so death spread to all men because all men sinned" (Rom. 5:12).

---
1 Taken from: http://www.reformed.org/documents/canons_of_orange.html

CANON 3. If anyone says that the grace of God can be conferred as a result of human prayer, but that it is not grace itself which makes us pray to God, he found by those who did not seek me; I have shown myself to those who did not ask for me" (Rom 10:20, quoting Isa. 65:1).

CANON 4. If anyone maintains that God awaits our will to be cleansed from sin, but does not confess that even our will to be cleansed comes to us through the infusion and working of the Holy Spirit, he resists the Holy Spirit himself who says through Solomon, "The will is prepared by the Lord" (Prov. 8:35, LXX), and the salutary word of the Apostle, "For God is at work in you, both to will and to work for his good pleasure" (Phil. 2:13).

CANON 5. If anyone says that not only the increase of faith but also its beginning and the very desire for faith, by which we believe in Him who justifies the ungodly and comes to the regeneration of holy baptism -- if anyone says that this belongs to us by nature and not by a gift of grace, that is, by the inspiration of the Holy Spirit amending our will and turning it from unbelief to faith and from godlessness to godliness, it is proof that he is opposed to the teaching of the Apostles, for blessed Paul says, "And I am sure that he who began a good work in you will bring it to completion at the day of Jesus Christ" (Phil. 1:6). And again, "For by grace you have been saved through faith; and this is not your own doing, it is the gift of God" (Eph. 2:8). For those who state that the faith by which we believe in God is natural make all who are separated from the Church of Christ by definition in some measure believers.

CANON 6. If anyone says that God has mercy upon us when, apart from his grace, we believe, will, desire, strive, labor, pray, watch, study, seek, ask, or knock, but does not confess that it is by the infusion and inspiration of the Holy Spirit within us that we have the faith, the will, or the strength to do all these things as we ought; or if anyone makes the assistance of grace depend on the humility or obedience of man and does not agree that it is a gift of grace itself that we are obedient and humble, he contradicts the Apostle who says, "What have you that you did not receive?" (1 Cor. 4:7), and, "But by the grace of God I am what I am" (1 Cor. 15:10).

CANON 7. If anyone affirms that we can form any right opinion or make any right choice which relates to the salvation of eternal life, as is expedient for us, or that we can be saved, that is, assent to the preaching of the gospel through our natural powers without the illumination and inspiration of the Holy Spirit, who makes all men gladly assent to and believe in the truth, he is led astray by a heretical spirit, and does not understand the voice of God who says in the Gospel, "For apart from me you can do nothing" (John 15:5), and the word of the Apostle, "Not that we are competent of ourselves to claim anything as coming from us; our competence is from God" (2 Cor. 3:5).

CANON 8. If anyone maintains that some are able to come to the grace of baptism by mercy but others through free will, which has manifestly been corrupted in all those who have been born after the transgression of the first man, it is proof that he has no place in the true faith. For he denies that the free will of all men has been weakened through the sin of the first man, or at least holds that it has been affected in such a way that they have still the ability to seek the mystery of eternal salvation by themselves without the revelation of God. The Lord himself shows how contradictory this is by declaring that no one is able to come to him "unless the Father who sent me draws him" (John 6:44), as he also says to Peter, "Blessed are you, Simon Bar-Jona! For flesh and blood has not revealed this to you, but my Father who is in heaven" (Matt. 16:17), and as the Apostle says, "No one can say 'Jesus is Lord' except by the Holy Spirit" (1 Cor. 12:3).

CANON 9. Concerning the succor of God. It is a mark of divine favor when we are of a right purpose and keep our feet from hypocrisy and unrighteousness; for as often as we do good, God is at work in us and with us, in order that we may do so.

CANON 10. Concerning the succor of God. The succor of God is to be ever sought by the regenerate and converted also, so that they may be able to come to a successful end or persevere in good works.

CANON 11. Concerning the duty to pray. None would make any true prayer to the Lord had he not received from him the object of his prayer, as it is written, "Of thy own have we given thee" (1 Chron. 29:14).

CANON 12. Of what sort we are whom God loves. God loves us for what we shall be by his gift, and not by our own deserving.

CANON 13. Concerning the restoration of free will. The freedom of will that was destroyed in the first man can be restored only by the grace of baptism, for what is lost can be returned only by the one who was able to give it. Hence the Truth itself declares: "So if the Son makes you free, you will be free indeed" (John 8:36).

CANON 14. No mean wretch is freed from his sorrowful state, however great it may be, save the one who is anticipated by the mercy of God, as the Psalmist says, "Let thy compassion come speedily to meet us" (Ps. 79:8), and again, "My God in his steadfast love will meet me" (Ps. 59:10).

CANON 15. Adam was changed, but for the worse, through his own iniquity from what God made him. Through the grace of God the believer is changed, but for the better, from what his iniquity has done for him. The one, therefore, was the change brought about by the first sinner; the other, according to the Psalmist, is the change of the right hand of the Most High (Ps. 77:10).

CANON 16. No man shall be honored by his seeming attainment, as though it were not a gift, or suppose that he has received it because a missive from without stated it in writing or in speech. For the Apostle speaks thus, "For if justification were through the law, then Christ died to no purpose" (Gal. 2:21); and "When he ascended on high he led a host of captives, and he gave gifts to men" (Eph. 4:8, quoting Ps. 68:18). It is from this source that any man has what he does; but whoever denies that he has it from this source either does not truly have it, or else "even what he has will be taken away" (Matt. 25:29).

CANON 17. Concerning Christian courage. The courage of the Gentiles is produced by simple greed, but the courage of Christians by the love of God which "has been poured into our hearts" not by freedom of will from our own side but "through the Holy Spirit which has been given to us" (Rom. 5:5).

CANON 18. That grace is not preceded by merit. Recompense is due to good works if they are performed; but grace, to which we have no claim, precedes them, to enable them to be done.

CANON 19. That a man can be saved only when God shows mercy. Human nature, even though it remained in that sound state in which it was created, could be no means save itself, without the assistance of the Creator; hence since man cannot safeguard his salvation without the grace of God, which is a gift, how will he be able to restore what he has lost without the grace of God?

CANON 20. That a man can do no good without God. God does much that is good in a man that the man does not do; but a man does nothing good for which God is not responsible, so as to let him do it.

CANON 21. Concerning nature and grace. As the Apostle most truly says to those who would be justified by the law and have fallen from grace, "If justification were through the law, then Christ died to no purpose" (Gal. 2:21), so it is most truly declared to those who imagine that grace, which faith in Christ advocates and lays hold of, is nature: "If justification were through nature, then Christ died to no purpose." Now there was indeed the law, but it did not justify, and there was indeed nature, but it did not justify. Not in vain did Christ therefore die, so that the law might be fulfilled by him who said, "I have come not to abolish them, but to fulfill them" (Matt. 5:17), and that the nature which had been destroyed by Adam might be restored by him who said that he had come "to seek and to save the lost" (Luke 19:10).

CANON 22. Concerning those things that belong to man. No man has anything of his own but untruth and sin. But if a man has any truth or righteousness, it from that fountain for which we must thirst in this desert, so that we may be refreshed from it as by drops of water and not faint on the way.

CANON 23. Concerning the will of God and of man. Men do their own will and not the will of God when they do what displeases him; but when they follow their own will and comply with the will of God, however willingly they do so, yet it is his will by which what they will is both prepared and instructed.

CANON 24. Concerning the branches of the vine. The branches on the vine do not give life to the vine, but receive life from it; thus the vine is related to its branches in such a way that it supplies them with what they need to live, and does not take this from them. Thus it is to the advantage of the disciples, not Christ, both to have Christ abiding in them and to abide in Christ. For if the vine is cut down another can shoot up from the live root; but one who is cut off from the vine cannot live without the root (John 15:5ff).

CANON 25. Concerning the love with which we love God. It is wholly a gift of God to love God. He who loves, even though he is not loved, allowed himself to be loved. We are loved, even when we displease him, so that we might have means to please him. For the Spirit, whom we love with the Father and the Son (Rom 5:5)

CONCLUSION. And thus according to the passages of holy scripture quoted above or the interpretations of the ancient Fathers we must, under the blessing of God, preach and believe as follows. The sin of the first man has so impaired and weakened free will that no one thereafter can either love God as he ought or believe in God or do good for God's sake, unless the grace of divine mercy has preceded him. We therefore believe that the glorious faith which was given to Abel the righteous, and Noah, and Abraham, and Isaac, and Jacob, and to all the saints of old, and which the Apostle Paul commends in extolling them (Heb. 11), was not given through natural goodness as it was before to Adam, but was bestowed by the grace of God. And we know and also believe that even after the coming of our Lord this grace is not to be found in the free will of all who desire to be baptized, but is bestowed by the kindness of Christ, as has already been frequently stated and as the Apostle Paul declares, "For it has been granted to you that for the sake of Christ you should not only believe in him but also suffer for his sake" (Phil. 1:29). And again, "He who began a good work in you will bring it to completion at the day of Jesus Christ" (Phil. 1:6). And again, "For by grace you have been saved through faith; and it is not your own doing, it is the gift of God" (Eph. 2:8). And as the Apostle says of himself, "I have obtained mercy to be faithful" (1 Cor. 7:25, cf. 1 Tim. 1:13). He did not say, "because I was faithful," but "to be faithful." And again, "What have you that you did not receive?" (1 Cor. 4:7). And again, "Every good endowment and every perfect gift is from above, coming down from the Father of lights" (Jas. 1:17). And again, "No one can receive anything except what is given him from heaven" (John 3:27). There are innumerable passages of holy scripture which can be quoted to prove the case for grace, but they have been omitted for the sake of brevity, because further examples will not really be of use where few are deemed sufficient.

According to the catholic faith we also believe that after grace has been received through baptism, all baptized persons have the ability and responsibility, if they desire to labor faithfully, to perform with the aid and cooperation of Christ what is of essential importance in regard to the salvation of their soul. We not only do not believe that any are foreordained to evil by the power of God, but even state with utter abhorrence that if there are those who want to believe so evil a thing, they are anathema. We also believe and confess to our benefit that in every good work it is not we who take the initiative and are then assisted through the mercy of God, but God himself first inspires in us both faith in him and love for him without any previous good works of our own that deserve reward, so that we may both faithfully seek the sacrament of baptism, and after baptism be able by his help to do what is pleasing to him. We must therefore most evidently believe that the praiseworthy faith of the thief whom the Lord called to his home in paradise, and of Cornelius the centurion, to whom the angel of the Lord was sent, and of Zacchaeus, who was worthy to receive the Lord himself, was not a natural endowment but a gift of God's kindness.

Key Terms for Humanity and Sin (1)

1. **Anthropology:** The study of the purpose and nature of humanity both in its pre-fall and post-fall state.
2. **Soul Sleep:** The belief that when people die their spirit/soul dies/sleeps also, with the result that they enter into a state of total unconsciousness until the resurrection.
3. **Monism:** The teaching that the spirit, soul, and body are all essentially the same or that the spirit and soul do not exist without the body. This often goes by the name "soul sleep."
4. **Dichotomy:** The belief that man consists of two essential parts: material (body) and immaterial (soul/spirit).
5. **Trichotomy:** The teaching that man is made up of three essential parts: body, soul, and spirit.
6. **Conditional Unity:** This position affirms both the essential unity of the material and immaterial part of man and the existence of an intermediate state. A person does not have a body and a soul, but is a body and a soul, neither of which alone make up the whole person.
7. **Gnostic Dualism:** The belief that man's constitution is physical and spiritual. The physical body is a burdensome temporary material confinement out of which we must escape.
8. **Creationism:** The belief that God creates each person's soul individually and then unites the soul to the body at conception, birth, or sometime in between.
9. **Pre-existence Theory:** The theory that people's souls/spirits preexisted the creation of their bodies. There may have been some former state in which the person sinned.
10. **Traducianism**: The belief that the soul is created in and with the body by the parents. While God is the ultimate creator of all things, he uses people intermediately or as secondary causes.
11. **Imago Dei:** The doctrine that man is created in the image of God.

Key Terms for Humanity and Sin (2)

1. **Original Sin:** A broad term that refers to the effects that the first sin had on humanity; the "origin" of sin.
2. **Imputed Sin:** Specifically refers to the guilt or condemnation of the first sin which was imputed to humanity. (Also: original guilt.)
3. **Inherited Sin:** Specifically refers to the transferal of the sinful nature. (Also: original corruption, original pollution, sinful nature.)
4. **Personal Sin:** Specifically refers to the sins that are committed by individuals.
5. **Pelagianism:** The belief that man is inherently good. The Fall not did bring condemnation upon any but Adam. As well, the disposition of the will is unaffected. Man sins as a result of bad examples that began with Adam.
6. **Fatalism**: Belief that a person's life and choices are totally and unalterably the result of an endless series of cause and effects.
7. **Compatibilism**: Belief that a person's actions are free, being determined by his or her own character and desires.
8. **Libertarianism:** Belief that a person's actions are uncaused by any coercion whatsoever. The agent is the "first cause" in the effect of his action.
9. **Egalitarianism:** Position that the Bible does not teach that women are in any sense, functionally or ontologically, subservient to men. Women and men hold ministry positions according to their gifts, not their gender. The principle of mutual submission teaches that husbands and wives are to submit to each other equally.
10. **Complementarianism:** Position that the Bible teaches that men and women are of equal worth, dignity, and responsibility before God (ontological equality). The Bible also teaches that men and women have different roles to play in society, the family, and the church. These roles do not compete but complement each other.

A CALVINIST'S UNDERSTANDING OF "FREE-WILL"

There are many words and concepts in theology that suffer from misunderstanding, mischaracterization, and misinformation. "Predestination," "Calvinism," "Total Depravity," "Inerrancy," and "Complementarianism", just to name a few that I personally have to deal with. Proponents are more often than not on the defensive, having to explain again and again why it is they don't mean what people think they mean.

The concept of "free will" suffers no less with regard to this misunderstanding. Does a person have free will? Well, what do you mean by "free will"? This must always be asked.

Do you mean:

1. That a person is not forced from the outside to make a choice?
2. That a person is responsible for his or her choices?
3. That a person is the active agent in a choice made?
4. That a person is free to do whatever they desire?
5. That a person has the ability to choose contrary to their nature (who they are)?

Calvinists, such as myself, do believe in free will and we don't believe in free will. It just depends on what you mean.

When it comes to the first three options, most Calvinist would agree that a person is not forced to make a choice, is responsible for their choices, and is the active agent behind those choices. They would reject the forth believing that a person is not free to do whatever they desire (for example, no matter how much one desires, he or she cannot read the thoughts of another person, fly without wings, or transport from one location to another just by thinking about the desired location).

It is important to note at this point, there is no conflict. No matter what theological persuasion you adhere to, most of historic Christianity has agreed that the first three are true, while the fourth is false.

It is with the fifth option there is disagreement.

Does a person have the ability to choose against their nature?

This question gets to the heart of the issue. Here we introduce a new and more defined term (hang with me here): "Libertarian Free-will" or "Libertarian Freedom." Libertarian freedom can be defined briefly thus:

Libertarian Freedom: "The power of contrary choice."

If you ask whether a person can choose against their nature (i.e. libertarian freedom) the answer, I believe, must be "no." A person's nature makes up who they are. Who they are determines their choice. If there choice is determined, then the freedom is self-limited. Therefore, there is no "power" of contrary choice for we cannot identify what or who this "power" might be. I know, I know . . . slow down. Let me explain.

First, it is important to get this out of the way. To associate this denial of libertarian freedom exclusively with Calvinism would be misleading. St. Augustine was the first to deal with this issue in a comprehensive manner. Until the forth century, it was simply assumed that people were free and responsible, but they had yet to flesh out what this meant. Augustine further elaborated on the Christian understanding of freedom. He argued that people choose according to who they are. If they are good, they make good choices. If they are bad, they make bad choices. These choices are free, they just lack liberty. In other words, a person does not become a sinner because they sin, they sin because they are a sinner. It is an issue of nature first. If people are identified with the fallen nature of Adam, then they will make choices similar to that of Adam because it is who they are. Yes, they are making a free choice, but this choice does not include the liberty or freedom of contrary choice.

What you have to ask is this: If "free will" means that we can choose against our nature (i.e. the power of contrary choice), if "free will" means that we can choose against who we are, what does this mean? What does this look like? How does a free person make a choice that is contrary to who they are? Who is actually making the choice? What is "free will" in this paradigm?

If one can choose according to who they are not, then they are not making the choice and this is not really freedom at all, no? Therefore, there is, at the very least, a self-determinism at work here. This is a limit on free will and, therefore, a necessary denial of true libertarian freedom.

Think about all that goes into making "who you are." We are born in the fallen line of Adam. Spiritually speaking we have an inbred inclination toward sin. All of our being is infected with sin. This is called "total depravity." Every aspect of our being is infected with sin, even if we don't act it out to a maximal degree.

But even if this were not the case,—even if total depravity were a false doctrine—libertarian freedom would still be untenable. Not only are you who you are because of your identification with a fallen human race, but notice all these factors that you did not choose that go into the set up for any given "free will" decision made:

* You did not choose when you were to be born.
* You did not choose where you were to be born.
* You did not choose your parents.
* You did not choose your influences early in your life.
* You did not choose whether you were to be male or female.
* You did not choose your genetics.
* You did not choose your temperament.
* You did not choose your looks.
* You did not choose your body type.
* You did not choose your physical abilities.

All of these factors play an influencing role in who you are at the time of any given decision. Yes, your choice is free, but it has you behind them. Therefore, you are free to choose according to you from whom you are not able to free yourself!

Now, I must reveal something here once again that might surprise many of you. This view is held by both Calvinists and Arminians alike. Neither position believes that a person can choose against their nature. Arminians, however, differ from Calvinists in that they believe in the doctrine of prevenient grace, which essentially neutralizes the will so that the inclination toward sin—the antagonism toward Gog—is relieved so that the person can make a true "free will" decision.

However, we still have some massive difficulties. Here are a couple:

A neutralized will amounts to your absence from the choice itself.

Changing the nature of a person so that their predispositions are neutral does not really help. We are back to the question What does a neutralized will look like? Does it erase all of the you behind the choice? If you are neutralized and liberated from you, then who is making the choice? How can you be held responsible for a choice that you did not really make, whether good or bad?

A neutralized will amounts to perpetual indecision. Think about this, if a person had true libertarian freedom, where there were no coercive forces, personal or divine, that influenced the decision, would a choice ever be made? If you have no reason to choose A or B, then neither would ever be chosen. Ronald Nash illustrates this by presenting a dog who has true libertarian freedom trying to decide between two bowls of dog food. He says that the dog would end up dying of starvation. Why? Because he would never have any reason to choose one over the other. It is like a balanced scale, it will never tilt to the right or the left unless the weights (influence) on one side is greater than the other. Then, no matter how little weight (influence) is added to a balanced scale, it will always choose accordingly.

A neutralized will amounts to arbitrary decisions, which one cannot be held responsible for.

For the sake of argument, let's say that libertarian choice could be made. Let's say that the dog did choose one food bowl over the other. In a truly libertarian sense, this decision cannot have influences of any kind. Any decision without influences is arbitrary. It would be like flipping a coin. I chose A rather than B, not because of who I am, but for no reason at all. It just turned out that way. But this option is clearly outside a biblical worldview of responsibility and judgment. Therefore, in my opinion, the outcome for the fight for true libertarian freewill comes at the expense of true responsibility!

In conclusion: while I believe in free will, I don't believe in libertarian free will. We make the choices we make because of who we are. We are responsible for these choices. God will judge each person accordingly with a righteous judgment.

Is there tension? Absolutely. We hold in tension our belief in God's sovereignty, determining who we are, when we live, where we will live, who our parents will be, our DNA, etc. and human responsibility. While this might seem uncomfortable, I believe that it is not only the best biblical option, but the only philosophical option outside outside of fatalism, and we don't want to go there.

Acts 17:26-28
"From one man he made every nation of men, that they should inhabit the whole earth; and he determined the times set for them and the exact places where they should live. 27 God did this so that men would seek him and perhaps reach out for him and find him, though he is not far from each one of us. 28 'For in him we live and move and have our being.'"

WHAT COMPLEMENTARIANISM IS REALLY ALL ABOUT

The most common understanding of both Complementarianism and Egalitarianism goes something like this:

Complementarians: Do not let women be pastors over men.

Egalitarians: Do let women be pastors over men.

or…

Complementarians: The husband is the leader of the family.

Egalitarians: The husband and wife co-lead the family, with no priority.

or…

Complementarians: Wives submit to your husbands.

Egalitarians: Husbands and wives are to practice mutual submission.

While I think that these are characteristics of both groups, they are not foundational characteristics that define each group. In other words, I don't think that they are helpful in defining what it means to be a complementarian or egalitarian and they serve to cause a great deal of misunderstanding that leads to emotional bias that is very difficult to overcome once set.

In fact, I am going to say something very radical here and then explain. Here it goes:

It is possible to be a complementarian and believe that a women can serve in the position of head pastor over men.

Did you get that? Reread it. Reread it again…

Complementarianism is not first defined by it view of the roles of men and women in the church, family, or society.

Here is what Complementarianism is:

Complementarianism is the belief that men and women have God given differences that are essential to their person. Men and women are ontologically (in their essential nature) equal, but often, functionally, take subordinate roles (like the Trinity). These differences complete or "complement" each other. Due to these differences, there will be some things that women are predisposed and purposed to do more than men. As well, there will be some things that men are predisposed and purposed to do more than women. Therefore, there are ideal roles for both men and women that should be celebrated, exemplified, typified, and promoted in the church, family, and society. To deny these differences is to deny the design of God and thwart his purpose.

Here is what Egalitarianism is:

The belief that God has created men and women equal in all things. Men and women are ontologically and functionally equal. The way the sexes function in the church, society, and the family is determined by individual giftedness, not role distinctions according to the sexes. Therefore, each person should be judged individually when being placed in a particular position. We should exemplify this reality by overcoming the stereotypical placement that has traditionally been a part of societies in human history, thereby giving freedom to individuals to follow the path that God has uniquely created them for, whatever that may be. In doing so, we should no longer educate or indoctrinate according to any of the former stereotypes, including those of basic masculinity and femininity.

These, in my opinion, are the foundational tenants of each position without giving examples on how this plays out in the family, the church, or society.

The case I am making here is that in order to be a consistent egalitarian, one must deny virtually all differences that typify men as men and women as women. It is not just about getting women behind the pulpit or the concept of mutual submission in the family. It is much more complex and, in my estimation, more difficult to defend with sensibility.

I had a professor at Dallas Theological Seminary who was an Egalitarian (he left because of this—I won't mention his name). I loved this guy. Still do. Great teacher, thinker, and Christian. In fact, I had him come speak to our pastoral staff at Stonebriar to challenge us on why he became egalitarian and to defend his position. I wanted the staff to understand the "other side" from a very able defender. During his presentation, he painted himself into this very typical corner that I find most all egalitarians end up.

He was advocating a foundational principle of egalitarianism: there are no essential differences between men and women other than reproductive stuff. We were all quite taken aback. Every example we brought up, he shot down by giving a counter-example in the form of an exception. His basic argument turned on finding exceptions to everything. Whether it was that men were less emotional, more aggressive, more one tracked in their thinking, less tender, more competitive, unable to nurture as well as women, or even liked the color blue more, he brought up exceptions that he believed neutralized the "pattern". Finally, I thought I had him. I said "What about physicality? Men are stronger than women." He would have none of that. He then brought up examples of German women who were stronger than men! We could not stump the guy!

The problem is that in order to defend egalitarianism consistently, he had to deny all of the common sense distinctions that people have made about men and women since the dawn of time. I won't get into the science or psychology of this issue as there are many very good resources that do this. To me, it is rather bizarre that one would actually be inclined to produce evidence to prove that men and women are different!

I am of the opinion that many egalitarians would have been appalled by Peter who said that women are the weaker of the sexes (1 Pet. 3:7) siting every exception to this rule and bemoaning this stereotype until Peter cried "uncle."

Complementarianism says that men and women are different by design. We are different and God did it. It is that simple.

However, most people would not be willing to go as far as my former professor. They realize that sustaining a proposition that men and women have no essential differences is a battle that cannot really be sustained in real life (only theoretical ideology). Men and women are different. Even most egalitarians that I know would give me this. Hear this again. Most egalitarians that I know would admit, when push comes to shove, that there are some essential differences between men and women. Most would even say that there are essential differences that go beyond reproduction and physicality. But I would argue that these people are not really egalitarians, at least in the way I have defined it. They would be complementarians because they would have given up what I believe to be a central driving tenant of egalitarianism and embraced the central tenant of complementarianism: men and women are different by design and their differences complement each other.

Now, having said this, I believe that it is theoretically possible to be a complementarian and yet not take a traditional complementarian stand on the issue of women in ministry. In other words, someone could believe that men and women are different by design yet not think that these differences have any bearing on women in leadership in the church. They may be convinced that the Bible does not really teach that women should not teach men, and yet be complementarian in other issues and, broadly, in their theology of the sexes.

I am interested and committed to complementarianism for more than just the women in ministry issue. This is just one application. But (and here is where I get in trouble with fellow complementarians), I don't think that it is the most important issue in this debate. Neither do I think that it is the most "damaging" issue.

You see, when people are truly committed and consistent egalitarians, they have to defend their denial of essential differences. In doing so, they will advocate a education system in the home, church, and society which neutralizes any assumption of differences between the sexes. In doing so, men will not be trained to be "men" since there is really no such thing. Women will not be encouraged to be "women" since there is no such thing. The assumption of differences becomes a way to oppress society and marginalize, in their estimation, one sex for the benefit of the other. Once we neutralize these differences, we will have neutered society and the family due to a denial of God's design in favor of some misguided attempt to promote a form of equality that is neither possible nor beneficial to either sex.

We will have troubled men and women groping to find their way and feeling pressured to repress their instincts and giftedness. We will no longer be able to train up men and women in the "way" they should go since there is no "way" they should go. Women can act masculine and men can be feminine. Men can retreat in the face of responsibility because, in truth, they don't have any "responsibility" other than the one that they choose. This is to say nothing of the implications this has on the issues of homosexuality and gay marriage.

But in a complementarian worldview (even one that allows women to teach men in the church), men are taught to be men and women are taught to be women. They both have defining characteristics. Masculinity and femininity find their place and are exemplified and celebrated. Men protect women from physical danger and take their positions of leadership seriously, without trepidation or fear that they will be seen as power mongers. And women support this. Women take up their positions of nurturing and supporting the emotional well-being of the world. And men support it. No role distinction is seen as inferior because in a complementarian worldview both are seen as essential and of equal importance. Only in complementarianism do we not define the rule by the exceptions and bow to the least common denominator. Only in the complementarian worldview, in my opinion, can freedom to be who we are supposed to be find meaning.

The true spirit of complementarianism is that God has intentionally created men and women with differences and we are to celebrate this in every way. The true spirit of complementarianism is never domineering (that is a sinful corruption). The true spirit of complementarianism provides no shame only freedom. The true spirit of complementarianism speaks to God in appreciation.

When we attempt to neuter this design, we have lost much more than authority in the pulpit.

Complementarians, while I believe that the Bible teaches the ideal that women should not have authority over men in the church, let us promote the true spirit of complementarianism then simply defending its particular applications.

WHY WOMEN CANNOT BE HEAD PASTORS

I don't know of many more controversial issues in the church than issues regarding women in ministry. It is not controversial whether or not women can do ministry or be effective in ministry, but whether or not they can teach and preside in positions of authority over men. The most controversial issue aspect of this issue, of course, is whether or not women can hold the position of head pastor or elder in a local church.

There are two primary positions in this debate; those who believe that women can teach men and hold positions of authority over men in the church and those that do not. Those that do, normally go by the name "Egalitarians." Those that do not, go by the name "Complementarians." I am a complementarian but I understand and appreciate the egalitarian position. In fact, the church I serve at most often is an egalitarian church. (However, I don't want you to think that my complementarianism is not important to me. There is much more to complementarianism than whether or not a woman can preach!)

There are a lot of passages of Scripture which contribute to the debate, but one stands out more than all the others. 1 Tim. 2:11-15:

"A woman must quietly receive instruction with entire submissiveness. 12 But I do not allow a woman to teach or exercise authority over a man, but to remain quiet. 13 For it was Adam who was first created, and then Eve. 14 And it was not Adam who was deceived, but the woman being deceived, fell into transgression. 15 But women will be preserved through the bearing of children if they continue in faith and love and sanctity with self-restraint."

I don't want to debate whether or not this passage teaches either position. I am simply going to assume the complementarian position and attempt to deal with the sting of "I don't allow a woman to teach." It does have quite a bit of sting.

I like to make the Scripture pragmatically understandable. In other words, I want to not only understand what it says, but to rationally understand why it says what it says. Why does God give this instruction or that? What practical rationale might be behind the instruction of God? I know that we cannot always find it and our obligation to obey transcends our understanding but, in my experience, more often than not, our understanding of the command can accompany our obedience so that we are not so blind.

"I do not allow a woman to teach." We think of this as coming from God. God says, "I do not allow a woman to teach." Teaching is something that requires _____ therefore, women are not qualified. You fill in the blank:

1. Intelligence

2. Wisdom

3. Love

4. Concern

5. Rational

6. Persuasiveness

While I think the sting of this passage assumes that Paul is speaking about one of these, I don't choose any of them. I think Paul (and God) has something different in mind.

The other night, at 3am there was a sound in our living room. Kristie woke up, but I did not. She was looking out there and saw the lights go on. She got scared.

Pop quiz: What did she do next?

a. Got a bat and quietly tip toed out there to see who it was.

b. Got a gun and peeked around the corner.

c. Woke me up and had me go out there.

Those of you who choose "c" are both right and wise. You are right because that is what happened. (It was my 2 year old Zach who decided it was time to get up.) You are wise because that is what normally happens and is typically, for those of you who have a man in the house, the best move. Why? Because men are better equipped to deal with these sort of situations. There is an aggression that men have, both physical and mental, that is more able to handle situations that might become combative. That is the way we are made.

Now, let me give my short and sweet answer as to why Paul did not allow women to teach:

Paul did not let women teach due to the often aggressive and combative nature that teaching must entail concerning the confrontation of false doctrine. Men must be the teachers when combating false teaching. However, because the role of a teacher in the church is so often to combat false doctrine, and because false doctrine is always a problem, generally speaking, the principles are always applicable. The "exercising of authority" is inherently tied to teaching and its necessary condemnation of false doctrine.

The combative nature of teaching is particularly relevant to a broader understanding of the characteristics of men and women.

The best illustration in the real world that I could use to help you understand what I am saying is that of a military commander in charge of leading troops into battle. Of course there might be an exception here and there, but do a study and you will find that no matter what the time or culture, men are always leading here. Why? Because men are simply better equipped and more followed. There are certian areas where men and women have a unique stature. I believe, like in military, the position of head pastor is the same. Not only are they better equipped for the issues that will arise, but they are followed more readily.

Let me give you another example: Two years ago, my wife was confronted by another couple who did not believe that she was doing what was right. She used to do princess parties where she would dress up as a princess (Cinderella, Snow White, Sleeping Beauty) and go to little girls' homes and entertain them for an hour or so. She was really good at this. After we moved from Frisco to Oklahoma, she still had one party on the schedule. She called her boss and let her know that she could not do it since we had already moved. Her boss became very angry and began to threaten her. She also said that she was going to bring in her husband (who was a lawyer) and sue Kristie. Kristie became very scared and did not know how to handle this situation, especially since her boss was now using her husband as part of the threat. She told me about this and I told her not to speak to her boss anymore, but to let me handle it. I did. I stepped in and confronted both her boss and her husband's threats concerning the issue. In the end, they backed off.

I felt that it was my duty and obligation to step in and be strong on behalf of my wife as the situation became confrontational. Kristie is both tender, gentle, and, in those situations, frightened. She was going to give in and travel back to Texas to perform this last party even though she would lose money in the gas it took to go there and back. Her boss refused to pay her mileage.

My point is that men are conditioned to handle confrontation better than women. It is not that Kristie could not have done the same thing as me, it is just that this was not her bent. Women, generally speaking, are not bent to deal with confrontation the same way as men. Teaching in the church involves, more often than not, confronting false understanding.

Can women teach? Absolutely! Can women understand and think as well as men? Most certainly. But the bent of a man is better able to handle the type of teaching that is always necessary in the church.

Would I let a woman teach from the pulpit from time to time? Yes. Paul is not restricting women teachers over men in the absolute sense. The infinitive here, "to teach" is in the present tense which suggests the perpetual role of teaching which exercises authority (confrontation).

The role of head pastor, I believe requires confrontation. That is not all there is, but it is there and it is very important. It is because of this, I believe, Paul said that women cannot teach or exercise authority over men.

159

THE PARABLE OF THE BOAT: ILLUSTRATING DIFFERENCES BETWEEN PELAGIANISM, SEMI-PELALGIANISM, EASTERN ORTHODOX, ROMAN CATHOLIC, ARMINIANISM, AND CALVINISM

Here is a quick illustration that I hope you find helpful to distinguish between the various traditions with regard to divine sovereignty, free-will, and salvation. It is certainly not perfect, but I think it works sufficiently.

Pelagianism

All the people are on the boat with the God. At this point, in their natural condition, they don't need to be saved as they are not in danger. However, most (if not all) people will eventually jump in the water (sin) and find themselves in need of God's grace. The reason why they jump in the water is because they are following numerous example of those who jumped before them. This example goes all the way back to the first two who jumped into the water, setting the first bad example. God them offers them a life preserver when they call on him for help. If they respond they will be saved (synergism).

Semi-Pelagianism

All people are in the water drowning. They are born drowning. This is the natural habitation of all humanity since the first man and woman jumped into the water. Their legs are cramping and they cannot swim to safety on their own. However, they may desire salvation on their own. Though they cannot attain it, they can call, with a wave of their arm, to God who is eagerly waiting on the edge of the boat. At the first sign of their initiative, God will then throw out the life preserver (grace). If they respond, they will be saved (synergism).

Roman Catholicism and Eastern Orthodoxy

All people are in the water drowning. They are born drowning. This is the natural habitation of all humanity since the first man and woman jumped into the water. Their legs are cramping and they cannot swim to safety on their own. God, standing on the edge of the boat, makes the first initiative by throwing a life preserver to them (prevenient grace). Upon seeing this act, they make a decision to grab a hold (faith) or to swim away. If they grab a hold, God will slowly pull the rope connected to the life preserver. But they must do their part by swimming along with God's pull (grace plus works; synergism). If at any time they let go or quit swimming, they will not be saved.

Arminianism

All people are floating in the water dead in their natural condition (total depravity). They are born dead because that has been the condition of humanity since the first man and woman jumped into the water and died (original sin). Death begets death. There must be intervention if they are to be saved. God uses his power to bring every one of them back to life (prevenient grace), but they are still in the water and in danger of drowning. With the regenerated ability to respond to God, now God throws the life preserver to them and calls on them all to grab hold of it. They then make the free-will decision on their own to grab a hold of the life preserver (faith) or to swim away. If they grab a hold, they must continue to hold as God pulls them in (synergism). They don't need to do anything but hold on. Any effort to swim and aid God is superfluous (sola fide). They can let go of the preserver at any time and, as a consequence, lose their salvation.

Calvinism

All people are floating in the water dead in their natural condition (total depravity). They are born dead because that has been the condition of humanity since the first man and woman jumped into the water and died (original sin). Death begets death. There must be radical intervention if they are to be saved. While God calls out to all of them (general call), due to his mysterious choice, he brings back to life (regeneration) only certain people (election) while passing by the rest (reprobation). He does not use a life preserver, but grabs a hold of the elect individually and immediately pulls them onto the boat (monergism).

They naturally grab a hold of God as a consequence of their regeneration (irresistible grace; sola fide). They forever stay on the boat due to their perpetual ability to recognize God's beauty (perseverance of the saints).

Made in the USA
Charleston, SC
10 December 2011